50 Sustainable Seafood Dish Recipes for Home

By: Kelly Johnson

Table of Contents

- Grilled Sustainable Salmon with Lemon Herb Butter
- Tuna Poke Bowl with Fresh Vegetables
- Oven-Roasted Whole Branzino with Mediterranean Herbs
- Seared Scallops with Citrus Salsa
- Shrimp Tacos with Avocado Crema
- Grilled Swordfish Steaks with Chimichurri Sauce
- Miso-glazed Black Cod
- Thai Coconut Curry Mussels
- Pan-Seared Sustainable Cod with Tomato Basil Relish
- Crab Cakes with Remoulade Sauce
- Baked Halibut with Garlic Parmesan Crust
- Grilled Octopus Salad with Cherry Tomatoes and Olives
- Salmon Burgers with Dill Aioli
- Ceviche with Fresh Local Fish
- Spicy Tuna Roll Sushi Bowl
- Coconut Lime Shrimp Skewers
- Fish Tacos with Mango Salsa
- Smoked Trout Pâté with Crostini
- Fisherman's Stew with Seasonal Seafood
- Grilled Sardines with Lemon and Garlic
- Lobster Risotto with Asparagus
- Lemon Herb Baked Rainbow Trout
- Tuna Nicoise Salad
- Clam Linguine with White Wine Sauce
- Seared Sea Bass with Herb Butter
- Grilled Mackerel with Roasted Vegetables
- Stuffed Squid with Mediterranean Couscous
- Salmon Teriyaki Skewers
- Scallop and Corn Chowder
- Baked Stuffed Shrimp with Herbed Crumbs
- Shrimp and Vegetable Stir-Fry
- Lemon Garlic Butter Crab Legs
- Grilled Mahi-Mahi Tacos with Pineapple Salsa
- Coconut-Crusted Shrimp with Mango Dipping Sauce
- Tuna Steaks with Sesame Ginger Glaze

- Smoked Haddock and Leek Gratin
- Paella with Sustainable Seafood Mix
- Grilled Calamari Salad with Fennel and Orange
- Crab-Stuffed Portobello Mushrooms
- Salmon Caesar Salad
- Thai Fish Curry with Seasonal Vegetables
- Grilled Shrimp and Vegetable Skewers
- Teriyaki Glazed Black Cod
- Smoked Salmon and Avocado Toast
- Pesto Grilled Shrimp Pasta
- Baked Stuffed Clams with Bacon
- Spicy Tuna Lettuce Wraps
- Mediterranean Tuna Salad
- Seared Ahi Tuna with Wasabi Aioli
- Baked Cod with Herbed Quinoa

Grilled Sustainable Salmon with Lemon Herb Butter

Ingredients:

- 4 sustainable salmon fillets (about 6 oz each)
- Salt and pepper, to taste
- Olive oil, for brushing

For the Lemon Herb Butter:

- 1/2 cup (1 stick) unsalted butter, softened
- Zest of 1 lemon
- 2 tablespoons fresh lemon juice
- 2 tablespoons finely chopped fresh parsley
- 1 tablespoon finely chopped fresh dill
- Salt and pepper, to taste

Instructions:

1. Prepare the Lemon Herb Butter:
   - In a small bowl, combine the softened butter, lemon zest, lemon juice, chopped parsley, chopped dill, salt, and pepper. Mix well until everything is thoroughly combined. You can adjust the seasoning to taste. Set aside.
2. Preheat the Grill:
   - Preheat your grill to medium-high heat. Make sure the grates are clean and lightly oiled to prevent sticking.
3. Season and Prepare the Salmon:
   - Pat the salmon fillets dry with paper towels. Season both sides of the salmon fillets with salt and pepper.
   - Brush the salmon lightly with olive oil to prevent sticking on the grill.
4. Grill the Salmon:
   - Place the salmon fillets directly on the preheated grill, skin-side down if the skin is on. Close the grill lid.
   - Grill the salmon for about 4-5 minutes per side, depending on the thickness of the fillets. The salmon is done when it easily flakes with a fork and is opaque in the center.
5. Serve:
   - Once the salmon is cooked through, carefully remove it from the grill and transfer to a serving platter.

- While the salmon is still hot, top each fillet with a generous dollop of the prepared lemon herb butter. The butter will melt and infuse the salmon with delicious flavor.
- Serve immediately with your choice of side dishes, such as grilled vegetables, rice, or a fresh green salad.

Tips:

- Use sustainably sourced salmon to support responsible fishing practices.
- Adjust the grilling time based on the thickness of your salmon fillets to avoid overcooking.
- You can add additional herbs or spices to the lemon herb butter based on your preference.
- Garnish with extra lemon wedges and fresh herbs for a beautiful presentation.

This Grilled Sustainable Salmon with Lemon Herb Butter is perfect for a weeknight dinner or a special occasion, offering a delightful combination of flavors that will impress your guests and family. Enjoy!

Tuna Poke Bowl with Fresh Vegetables

Ingredients:

- 1 lb fresh sushi-grade tuna, cubed
- 2 tablespoons soy sauce
- 1 tablespoon sesame oil
- 1 teaspoon rice vinegar
- 1 teaspoon honey or maple syrup
- 1 teaspoon sriracha (optional, for a spicy kick)
- 2 green onions, thinly sliced
- 1 avocado, diced
- 1 cucumber, thinly sliced
- 1 carrot, shredded
- 1 red bell pepper, thinly sliced
- 1 cup cooked sushi rice or brown rice
- 1 tablespoon sesame seeds, for garnish
- Fresh cilantro or microgreens, for garnish
- Lime wedges, for serving

Instructions:

1. Prepare the Tuna:
    - In a mixing bowl, combine the cubed tuna with soy sauce, sesame oil, rice vinegar, honey (or maple syrup), and sriracha (if using). Toss gently to coat the tuna. Cover and refrigerate while you prepare the other ingredients.
2. Prepare the Vegetables:
    - Prepare all the vegetables by slicing, dicing, and shredding them as indicated in the ingredients list. Arrange them in separate bowls for easy assembly.
3. Cook the Rice:
    - Cook the sushi rice or brown rice according to package instructions. Once cooked, let it cool slightly before assembling the poke bowls.
4. Assemble the Poke Bowls:
    - Divide the cooked rice among serving bowls.
    - Top each bowl with marinated tuna cubes.
    - Arrange the diced avocado, sliced cucumber, shredded carrot, and sliced red bell pepper around the tuna.
5. Garnish and Serve:
    - Sprinkle each bowl with sliced green onions and sesame seeds.

- Garnish with fresh cilantro or microgreens.
- Serve the tuna poke bowls immediately with lime wedges on the side.

Tips:

- Use the freshest sushi-grade tuna available for the best flavor and texture.
- Customize the vegetables based on your preferences. You can also add ingredients like edamame, radishes, or seaweed salad.
- Adjust the level of spiciness by adding more or less sriracha to the tuna marinade.
- Drizzle extra soy sauce or sesame oil over the assembled poke bowls for extra flavor, if desired.
- Enjoy your tuna poke bowls fresh for optimal taste and texture.

This Tuna Poke Bowl with Fresh Vegetables is a delightful and nutritious meal that's perfect for lunch or dinner. It's light, refreshing, and bursting with flavors. Feel free to get creative with the ingredients and enjoy this dish with your favorite toppings!

Oven-Roasted Whole Branzino with Mediterranean Herbs

Ingredients:

- 2 whole Branzino (about 1 pound each), scaled and gutted
- Salt and pepper, to taste
- 2 tablespoons extra virgin olive oil
- 2 cloves garlic, thinly sliced
- 1 lemon, thinly sliced
- 1 tablespoon chopped fresh rosemary
- 1 tablespoon chopped fresh thyme
- 1 tablespoon chopped fresh parsley
- 1/2 teaspoon paprika (optional)
- Lemon wedges, for serving
- Fresh herbs for garnish (rosemary sprigs, parsley)

Instructions:

1. Preheat the Oven:
    - Preheat your oven to 400°F (200°C).
2. Prepare the Branzino:
    - Rinse the Branzino under cold water and pat dry with paper towels.
    - Using a sharp knife, make 2-3 diagonal cuts on each side of the fish (this helps the fish cook evenly and allows the flavors to penetrate).
3. Season the Fish:
    - Season the inside and outside of the Branzino generously with salt and pepper.
4. Stuff the Fish:
    - Stuff the cavity of each fish with lemon slices, garlic slices, and a mixture of chopped fresh herbs (rosemary, thyme, parsley).
5. Drizzle with Olive Oil:
    - Place the Branzino on a baking sheet lined with parchment paper or aluminum foil. Drizzle each fish with olive oil, ensuring they are well coated.
6. Season and Bake:
    - Sprinkle paprika (if using), additional salt, and pepper over the fish.
    - Bake in the preheated oven for 20-25 minutes, or until the flesh is opaque and easily flakes with a fork. Cooking time may vary depending on the size of the fish.
7. Serve:

- Carefully transfer the roasted Branzino to serving plates.
- Garnish with fresh herbs and serve with lemon wedges on the side.

Tips:

- Choose fresh, high-quality Branzino for the best flavor. Ask your fishmonger to clean and scale the fish for you.
- Feel free to customize the herb stuffing based on your preference. You can use other Mediterranean herbs like oregano or basil.
- Serve the roasted Branzino with a side of roasted vegetables, couscous, or a simple green salad for a complete meal.
- Drizzle a little more olive oil or a squeeze of fresh lemon juice over the fish just before serving for extra flavor.

This oven-roasted whole Branzino with Mediterranean herbs is a perfect dish for a special dinner. The combination of aromatic herbs, garlic, and lemon complements the mild and delicate flavor of the Branzino beautifully. Enjoy this Mediterranean-inspired seafood dish with family and friends!

Seared Scallops with Citrus Salsa

Ingredients:

For the Scallops:

- 12 large sea scallops, side muscle removed
- Salt and pepper, to taste
- 2 tablespoons olive oil
- 1 tablespoon unsalted butter

For the Citrus Salsa:

- 1 orange, peeled and diced
- 1 grapefruit, peeled and diced
- 1 lime, juiced
- 2 tablespoons finely chopped red onion
- 1 tablespoon chopped fresh cilantro
- 1 tablespoon chopped fresh mint
- Salt and pepper, to taste

Instructions:

1. Prepare the Citrus Salsa:
    - In a bowl, combine the diced orange, diced grapefruit, lime juice, chopped red onion, chopped cilantro, and chopped mint.
    - Season the salsa with salt and pepper to taste. Set aside to let the flavors meld while you cook the scallops.
2. Prepare and Cook the Scallops:
    - Pat the scallops dry with paper towels. Season both sides of the scallops with salt and pepper.
    - In a large skillet, heat the olive oil over medium-high heat.
    - Add the butter to the skillet. Once the butter is melted and the pan is hot, carefully add the scallops in a single layer, making sure they are not too crowded.
    - Sear the scallops for about 2-3 minutes on each side, or until they develop a golden-brown crust and are cooked through. Be careful not to overcook them as they can become tough.
3. Serve:
    - Arrange the seared scallops on serving plates.

- Spoon the citrus salsa over the scallops or serve it on the side.
- Garnish with additional fresh herbs, if desired.

Tips:

- Use fresh and dry scallops for the best results. Patting them dry before cooking helps achieve a nice sear.
- Make sure the skillet is hot before adding the scallops to ensure a good sear.
- Feel free to customize the citrus salsa by adding diced avocado, jalapeño for heat, or other favorite ingredients.
- Serve the seared scallops with a side of couscous, rice, or a simple green salad for a complete meal.

This Seared Scallops with Citrus Salsa dish is elegant and bursting with refreshing flavors. It's perfect for a special dinner or when you want to impress guests with a restaurant-quality seafood dish at home. Enjoy!

Shrimp Tacos with Avocado Crema

Ingredients:

For the Shrimp:

- 1 lb large shrimp, peeled and deveined
- 1 tablespoon olive oil
- 1 teaspoon chili powder
- 1/2 teaspoon cumin
- Salt and pepper, to taste
- Juice of 1 lime

For the Avocado Crema:

- 1 ripe avocado
- 1/2 cup sour cream or Greek yogurt
- Juice of 1 lime
- 1 garlic clove, minced
- Salt and pepper, to taste

For Serving:

- Corn or flour tortillas
- Shredded cabbage or lettuce
- Sliced radishes
- Chopped cilantro
- Sliced jalapeños (optional)
- Lime wedges

Instructions:

1. Prepare the Avocado Crema:
    - In a blender or food processor, combine the avocado, sour cream (or Greek yogurt), lime juice, minced garlic, salt, and pepper.
    - Blend until smooth and creamy. Adjust seasoning to taste. Transfer the avocado crema to a bowl and set aside.
2. Prepare the Shrimp:

- In a bowl, combine the shrimp with olive oil, chili powder, cumin, salt, pepper, and lime juice. Toss to coat the shrimp evenly.
- Heat a skillet or grill pan over medium-high heat. Add the seasoned shrimp and cook for 2-3 minutes per side, or until the shrimp are pink and opaque. Remove from heat.

3. Assemble the Shrimp Tacos:
    - Warm the tortillas in a dry skillet or microwave.
    - Spread a spoonful of avocado crema on each tortilla.
    - Top with cooked shrimp, shredded cabbage or lettuce, sliced radishes, chopped cilantro, and sliced jalapeños (if using).
    - Serve the shrimp tacos with lime wedges on the side.

Tips:

- Choose fresh, large shrimp for the best flavor and texture.
- Customize the seasoning of the shrimp based on your preference. You can add more spice with cayenne pepper or chipotle powder.
- If you prefer a spicier avocado crema, add a dash of hot sauce or finely chopped jalapeño.
- Serve the shrimp tacos with your favorite side dishes like Mexican rice, refried beans, or a corn salad.

These Shrimp Tacos with Avocado Crema are quick and easy to make, yet full of vibrant flavors and textures. They're perfect for a weeknight dinner or a casual gathering with friends and family. Enjoy the delicious combination of tender shrimp, creamy avocado crema, and fresh toppings wrapped in warm tortillas!

Grilled Swordfish Steaks with Chimichurri Sauce

Ingredients:

For the Swordfish Steaks:

- 4 swordfish steaks, about 6-8 oz each
- Salt and pepper, to taste
- Olive oil, for brushing

For the Chimichurri Sauce:

- 1 cup fresh parsley, finely chopped
- 1/4 cup fresh cilantro, finely chopped
- 3 garlic cloves, minced
- 1 shallot, finely chopped
- 1/4 cup red wine vinegar
- 1/2 cup extra virgin olive oil
- 1 teaspoon dried oregano
- 1/2 teaspoon red pepper flakes (adjust to taste)
- Salt and pepper, to taste
- Juice of 1/2 lemon (optional)

Instructions:

1. Prepare the Chimichurri Sauce:
    - In a bowl, combine the finely chopped parsley, cilantro, minced garlic, chopped shallot, red wine vinegar, extra virgin olive oil, dried oregano, red pepper flakes, salt, and pepper.
    - Mix well to combine all the ingredients. Taste and adjust seasoning as needed.
    - If desired, add the juice of half a lemon to brighten the flavors. Set the chimichurri sauce aside to let the flavors meld while you prepare the swordfish.
2. Prepare and Grill the Swordfish:
    - Preheat your grill to medium-high heat.
    - Pat the swordfish steaks dry with paper towels. Season both sides of the steaks with salt and pepper.

- Brush the swordfish steaks lightly with olive oil to prevent sticking on the grill.
- Place the swordfish steaks on the preheated grill. Grill for about 4-5 minutes per side, depending on the thickness of the steaks, or until the fish is cooked through and has grill marks. Avoid overcooking to keep the swordfish moist and tender.

3. Serve:
    - Remove the grilled swordfish steaks from the grill and transfer them to a serving platter.
    - Spoon the chimichurri sauce generously over the swordfish steaks.
    - Serve immediately with additional chimichurri sauce on the side.

Tips:

- Choose fresh and sustainably sourced swordfish for the best flavor and quality.
- If you don't have a grill, you can also cook the swordfish steaks in a hot skillet on the stovetop or under the broiler in the oven.
- Feel free to customize the chimichurri sauce by adjusting the amount of garlic, red pepper flakes, or vinegar based on your taste preferences.
- Serve the grilled swordfish steaks with your favorite side dishes such as roasted vegetables, couscous, or a fresh green salad.

Grilled swordfish steaks with chimichurri sauce are a fantastic option for a special dinner or outdoor barbecue. The vibrant flavors of the chimichurri sauce complement the rich and meaty swordfish beautifully. Enjoy this delicious and elegant seafood dish!

Miso-glazed Black Cod

Ingredients:

- 4 black cod fillets, skin-on (about 6 oz each)
- Salt and pepper, to taste
- 1/4 cup white miso paste
- 2 tablespoons mirin (Japanese sweet rice wine)
- 2 tablespoons sake (Japanese rice wine)
- 2 tablespoons brown sugar
- 1 tablespoon soy sauce
- 1 teaspoon grated fresh ginger
- 1 clove garlic, minced
- Sesame seeds, for garnish (optional)
- Sliced green onions, for garnish (optional)

Instructions:

1. Prepare the Miso Glaze:
    - In a small saucepan, combine the white miso paste, mirin, sake, brown sugar, soy sauce, grated ginger, and minced garlic.
    - Heat the mixture over medium heat, stirring constantly until the sugar is dissolved and the mixture is smooth. Remove from heat and let it cool slightly.
2. Marinate the Black Cod:
    - Pat the black cod fillets dry with paper towels. Season both sides of the fillets with salt and pepper.
    - Place the fillets in a shallow dish or a resealable plastic bag.
    - Pour the cooled miso glaze over the black cod fillets, making sure they are evenly coated. Cover the dish or seal the bag, then refrigerate for at least 1 hour, or up to 24 hours for maximum flavor.
3. Preheat the Oven:
    - Preheat your oven to 400°F (200°C).
4. Cook the Black Cod:
    - Remove the marinated black cod fillets from the refrigerator and let them come to room temperature for about 15 minutes.
    - Place the fillets on a baking sheet lined with parchment paper, skin-side down.
    - Spoon any remaining miso glaze over the fillets.

- Bake the black cod in the preheated oven for 12-15 minutes, or until the fish is opaque and flakes easily with a fork. The edges should be caramelized and slightly golden.

5. Serve:
    - Carefully transfer the miso-glazed black cod fillets to serving plates.
    - Garnish with sesame seeds and sliced green onions, if desired.
    - Serve immediately, preferably with steamed rice and your favorite vegetables.

Tips:

- Choose high-quality black cod fillets for the best results. The skin-on fillets will help protect the delicate flesh during cooking.
- Adjust the sweetness of the miso glaze by adding more or less brown sugar, according to your taste preference.
- Be cautious not to overcook the black cod, as it can become dry. It's best to check for doneness by gently flaking the fish with a fork.
- If you prefer grilling, you can grill the miso-glazed black cod over medium-high heat for a smoky flavor.

Miso-glazed black cod is a restaurant-quality dish that you can easily prepare at home. Enjoy the rich, savory-sweet flavors of this delicious seafood dish with your family and friends!

Thai Coconut Curry Mussels

Ingredients:

- 2 pounds fresh mussels, cleaned and debearded
- 1 tablespoon vegetable oil
- 1 small onion, finely chopped
- 3 cloves garlic, minced
- 1 tablespoon grated ginger
- 2 tablespoons Thai red curry paste (adjust to taste for spice level)
- 1 can (13.5 oz) coconut milk
- 1 tablespoon fish sauce
- 1 tablespoon soy sauce
- 1 tablespoon brown sugar (or palm sugar)
- Juice of 1 lime
- Fresh cilantro leaves, chopped (for garnish)
- Thai basil leaves, torn (for garnish)
- Cooked jasmine rice or crusty bread (for serving)

Instructions:

1. Prepare the Mussels:
    - Rinse the fresh mussels under cold running water, scrubbing them with a brush to remove any dirt or debris. Pull off the beards (the fibrous threads) and discard any mussels that are open and do not close when tapped.
2. Cook the Aromatics:
    - In a large pot or Dutch oven, heat the vegetable oil over medium heat. Add the chopped onion and cook until softened and translucent, about 3-4 minutes.
    - Stir in the minced garlic and grated ginger, and cook for another 1-2 minutes until fragrant.
3. Add the Curry Paste and Coconut Milk:
    - Add the Thai red curry paste to the pot, stirring to coat the aromatics. Cook for 1 minute to release the flavors of the curry paste.
    - Pour in the coconut milk, fish sauce, soy sauce, and brown sugar. Stir well to combine and bring the mixture to a simmer.
4. Cook the Mussels:
    - Add the cleaned mussels to the pot, stirring gently to coat them in the curry coconut broth.

- Cover the pot with a lid and let the mussels cook for 5-7 minutes, or until all the mussels have opened. Discard any mussels that have not opened after cooking.
5. Finish and Serve:
    - Squeeze the juice of one lime into the pot and give it a final stir.
    - Taste the broth and adjust the seasoning with more fish sauce, soy sauce, brown sugar, or lime juice if needed.
    - Remove the pot from the heat and sprinkle chopped cilantro and torn Thai basil leaves over the mussels.
    - Serve the Thai coconut curry mussels hot with cooked jasmine rice or crusty bread on the side.

Tips:

- Use fresh and live mussels for the best flavor and texture. Discard any mussels that do not close when tapped or any mussels that remain closed after cooking.
- Adjust the amount of Thai red curry paste based on your spice preference. Start with a smaller amount and add more if you like it spicier.
- Garnish the mussels with additional fresh herbs like Thai basil, sliced red chilies, or chopped scallions for extra flavor and freshness.
- Enjoy the Thai coconut curry mussels immediately as a main dish or appetizer. Serve with rice or bread to soak up the delicious broth.

This Thai coconut curry mussels recipe is perfect for seafood lovers and those who enjoy Thai-inspired flavors. It's a comforting and satisfying dish that's sure to impress your family and guests!

Pan-Seared Sustainable Cod with Tomato Basil Relish

Ingredients:

For the Pan-Seared Cod:

- 4 sustainable cod fillets (about 6 oz each), skinless
- Salt and pepper, to taste
- 2 tablespoons olive oil
- 2 tablespoons unsalted butter
- Lemon wedges, for serving

For the Tomato Basil Relish:

- 2 cups cherry tomatoes, halved
- 1/4 cup fresh basil leaves, thinly sliced
- 2 tablespoons extra virgin olive oil
- 1 tablespoon balsamic vinegar
- 1 garlic clove, minced
- Salt and pepper, to taste

Instructions:

1. Prepare the Tomato Basil Relish:
   - In a medium bowl, combine the cherry tomatoes, sliced basil, extra virgin olive oil, balsamic vinegar, minced garlic, salt, and pepper. Toss gently to combine. Set aside to marinate while you cook the cod.
2. Cook the Cod:
   - Pat the cod fillets dry with paper towels. Season both sides of the cod fillets with salt and pepper.
   - In a large skillet, heat the olive oil and butter over medium-high heat.
   - Once the skillet is hot, add the cod fillets to the skillet. Cook for about 4-5 minutes on the first side, without moving them, until golden brown and easily release from the pan.
   - Carefully flip the cod fillets and cook for another 3-4 minutes on the second side, or until the fish is opaque and flakes easily with a fork.
3. Serve:
   - Transfer the cooked cod fillets to serving plates.
   - Spoon the tomato basil relish generously over the cod fillets.

- Serve immediately with lemon wedges on the side.

Tips:

- Choose sustainably sourced cod for this recipe to support responsible fishing practices.
- Adjust the cooking time based on the thickness of your cod fillets to ensure they are cooked through but not overcooked.
- Feel free to customize the tomato basil relish by adding diced red onion, capers, or olives for additional flavor and texture.
- Serve the pan-seared cod with a side of steamed vegetables, roasted potatoes, or a fresh green salad for a complete meal.

This pan-seared sustainable cod with tomato basil relish is a perfect dish for a quick and elegant dinner. The combination of flaky cod and bright, herbaceous tomato relish creates a delightful harmony of flavors. Enjoy this delicious seafood meal with your family and friends!

Crab Cakes with Remoulade Sauce

Ingredients:

For the Crab Cakes:

- 1 pound lump crab meat, picked over for shells
- 1/2 cup breadcrumbs
- 1/4 cup mayonnaise
- 1 large egg, beaten
- 2 tablespoons Dijon mustard
- 2 green onions, finely chopped
- 2 tablespoons chopped fresh parsley
- 1 tablespoon lemon juice
- 1 teaspoon Old Bay seasoning (or seafood seasoning)
- Salt and pepper, to taste
- 1/4 cup flour, for coating
- 2-3 tablespoons olive oil or vegetable oil, for frying

For the Remoulade Sauce:

- 1/2 cup mayonnaise
- 2 tablespoons Dijon mustard
- 2 tablespoons chopped pickles or cornichons
- 1 tablespoon capers, drained and chopped
- 1 tablespoon chopped fresh parsley
- 1 tablespoon chopped fresh chives or green onions
- 1 tablespoon lemon juice
- 1 teaspoon Worcestershire sauce
- 1/2 teaspoon hot sauce (adjust to taste)
- Salt and pepper, to taste

Instructions:

1. Prepare the Remoulade Sauce:
    - In a bowl, combine all the remoulade sauce ingredients - mayonnaise, Dijon mustard, chopped pickles, capers, chopped parsley, chopped chives or green onions, lemon juice, Worcestershire sauce, hot sauce, salt, and pepper. Mix well to combine. Taste and adjust seasoning according to your preference. Cover and refrigerate until ready to serve.

2. Make the Crab Cakes:
   - In a large bowl, gently combine the lump crab meat, breadcrumbs, mayonnaise, beaten egg, Dijon mustard, chopped green onions, chopped parsley, lemon juice, Old Bay seasoning, salt, and pepper. Be careful not to break up the crab meat too much.
   - Divide the mixture into equal portions and shape each portion into a patty (about 1/2-inch thick). Coat each crab cake lightly in flour, shaking off any excess.
3. Cook the Crab Cakes:
   - Heat olive oil or vegetable oil in a large skillet over medium-high heat.
   - Add the crab cakes to the skillet (you may need to cook them in batches to avoid overcrowding) and cook for about 3-4 minutes on each side, or until golden brown and crispy. Use a spatula to carefully flip the crab cakes.
4. Serve:
   - Transfer the cooked crab cakes to a serving platter.
   - Serve the crab cakes hot with a dollop of remoulade sauce on top or on the side.
   - Garnish with additional chopped parsley or chives, if desired.
   - Enjoy your delicious crab cakes with remoulade sauce as an appetizer or main course!

Tips:

- Use high-quality lump crab meat for the best flavor and texture.
- Feel free to add extra seasoning or herbs to the crab cake mixture based on your taste preferences.
- Serve the crab cakes with a side salad, coleslaw, or roasted vegetables for a complete meal.
- The remoulade sauce can be made ahead of time and refrigerated until ready to use. Stir well before serving.

These crab cakes with remoulade sauce are sure to be a hit at your next gathering or family dinner. They're flavorful, crispy, and perfect for seafood lovers!

Baked Halibut with Garlic Parmesan Crust

Ingredients:

- 4 halibut fillets (about 6 oz each), skin removed
- Salt and pepper, to taste
- 2 tablespoons butter, melted
- 2 cloves garlic, minced
- 1/2 cup grated Parmesan cheese
- 1/4 cup panko breadcrumbs (or regular breadcrumbs)
- 1 tablespoon chopped fresh parsley
- Lemon wedges, for serving

Instructions:

1. Preheat the Oven:
    - Preheat your oven to 400°F (200°C). Lightly grease a baking dish or line it with parchment paper.
2. Prepare the Halibut Fillets:
    - Pat the halibut fillets dry with paper towels. Season both sides of the fillets with salt and pepper.
    - Place the seasoned halibut fillets in the prepared baking dish, leaving space between each fillet.
3. Make the Garlic Parmesan Crust:
    - In a small bowl, combine the melted butter and minced garlic.
    - In another bowl, mix together the grated Parmesan cheese, panko breadcrumbs, and chopped fresh parsley.
4. Assemble and Bake:
    - Brush the tops of the halibut fillets with the garlic butter mixture, ensuring they are evenly coated.
    - Press the Parmesan breadcrumb mixture onto the tops of each halibut fillet, creating a thick crust.
    - Bake the halibut in the preheated oven for 12-15 minutes, or until the fish is opaque and flakes easily with a fork, and the crust is golden brown and crispy.
5. Serve:
    - Remove the baked halibut fillets from the oven and let them rest for a few minutes.
    - Carefully transfer the halibut fillets to serving plates.
    - Serve hot with lemon wedges on the side for squeezing over the fish.

Tips:

- Choose fresh and high-quality halibut fillets for the best results.
- Adjust the amount of garlic and Parmesan cheese in the crust based on your taste preference.
- If you don't have panko breadcrumbs, regular breadcrumbs will work fine.
- Garnish the baked halibut with additional chopped parsley or a sprinkle of grated Parmesan cheese before serving.
- Serve the baked halibut with a side of roasted vegetables, steamed asparagus, or a fresh green salad for a complete meal.

This baked halibut with garlic parmesan crust is a delightful and elegant dish that's sure to impress your family and guests. Enjoy the tender, flaky halibut with its flavorful crust for a delicious seafood dinner!

Grilled Octopus Salad with Cherry Tomatoes and Olives

Ingredients:

For Grilling the Octopus:

- 1 large octopus (about 2-3 pounds), cleaned and prepared
- 2 tablespoons olive oil
- Salt and pepper, to taste
- Juice of 1 lemon

For the Salad:

- 1 pint cherry tomatoes, halved
- 1/2 cup pitted Kalamata olives, halved
- 1/4 cup red onion, thinly sliced
- 2 tablespoons chopped fresh parsley
- 2 tablespoons chopped fresh basil
- 2 tablespoons extra virgin olive oil
- 1 tablespoon red wine vinegar
- Salt and pepper, to taste
- Lemon wedges, for serving

Instructions:

1. Prepare and Grill the Octopus:
    - Preheat a grill or grill pan over medium-high heat.
    - Pat the octopus dry with paper towels. Rub the octopus with olive oil and season generously with salt and pepper.
    - Place the octopus on the preheated grill and cook for about 20-30 minutes, turning occasionally, until the octopus is tender and charred in spots. The cooking time will depend on the size of the octopus. You can test for doneness by inserting a fork into the thickest part of the tentacle - it should be tender and easily pierced.
    - Remove the octopus from the grill and let it cool slightly. Slice the octopus into bite-sized pieces.
2. Assemble the Salad:
    - In a large bowl, combine the sliced octopus pieces, halved cherry tomatoes, halved Kalamata olives, thinly sliced red onion, chopped parsley, and chopped basil.

- In a separate small bowl, whisk together the extra virgin olive oil, red wine vinegar, salt, and pepper to make the dressing.
- Pour the dressing over the octopus and vegetable mixture. Toss gently to combine and coat everything evenly with the dressing.

3. Serve:
    - Arrange the grilled octopus salad on a serving platter or individual plates.
    - Garnish with additional chopped herbs, if desired.
    - Serve the salad with lemon wedges on the side for squeezing over the salad just before eating.

Tips:

- If octopus is not readily available or you prefer a quicker option, you can use pre-cooked octopus or substitute with grilled shrimp or calamari for a similar Mediterranean salad.
- Feel free to add other ingredients to the salad such as diced cucumber, bell peppers, or feta cheese for additional flavor and texture.
- Make sure to adjust the seasoning of the salad dressing according to your taste preference.
- This salad can be served as an appetizer, side dish, or light main course. Enjoy it with crusty bread or alongside grilled vegetables.

Grilled octopus salad with cherry tomatoes and olives is a delightful and vibrant dish that's perfect for summer gatherings or as a light and refreshing meal any time of the year. Enjoy the combination of tender octopus, juicy cherry tomatoes, and briny olives in every bite!

Salmon Burgers with Dill Aioli

Ingredients:

For the Salmon Burgers:

- 1 pound fresh salmon fillet, skin removed
- 1/4 cup panko breadcrumbs
- 1/4 cup finely chopped red onion
- 2 tablespoons chopped fresh dill
- 1 tablespoon Dijon mustard
- 1 tablespoon mayonnaise
- 1 tablespoon lemon juice
- Salt and pepper, to taste
- Olive oil, for cooking
- Burger buns or lettuce wraps, for serving

For the Dill Aioli:

- 1/2 cup mayonnaise
- 1 tablespoon chopped fresh dill
- 1 tablespoon lemon juice
- 1 garlic clove, minced
- Salt and pepper, to taste

Optional Burger Toppings:

- Sliced tomato
- Red onion slices
- Lettuce leaves
- Pickles

Instructions:

1. Prepare the Salmon Patties:
    - Cut the salmon fillet into small chunks. Place the salmon chunks in a food processor and pulse a few times until coarsely ground. Be careful not to over-process; you want some texture remaining.

- In a mixing bowl, combine the ground salmon, panko breadcrumbs, chopped red onion, chopped fresh dill, Dijon mustard, mayonnaise, lemon juice, salt, and pepper. Mix until well combined.

2. Form the Salmon Burgers:
    - Divide the salmon mixture into 4 equal portions. Shape each portion into a patty, about 1/2-inch thick. Place the patties on a plate lined with parchment paper.
3. Make the Dill Aioli:
    - In a small bowl, whisk together the mayonnaise, chopped fresh dill, lemon juice, minced garlic, salt, and pepper until smooth and well combined. Adjust seasoning to taste. Cover and refrigerate until ready to use.
4. Cook the Salmon Burgers:
    - Heat a drizzle of olive oil in a skillet over medium-high heat.
    - Add the salmon patties to the skillet and cook for about 3-4 minutes per side, or until golden brown and cooked through. The internal temperature of the salmon should reach 145°F (63°C).
5. Assemble the Salmon Burgers:
    - Toast the burger buns lightly if desired.
    - Spread a generous amount of dill aioli on both sides of each burger bun.
    - Place a salmon patty on the bottom half of each bun.
    - Top with sliced tomato, red onion, lettuce leaves, or your favorite burger toppings.
    - Cover with the top half of the burger bun.
6. Serve and Enjoy:
    - Serve the salmon burgers immediately, accompanied by additional dill aioli on the side if desired.
    - Enjoy these delicious salmon burgers with a side salad, coleslaw, or sweet potato fries.

Tips:

- Choose fresh, high-quality salmon for the best flavor and texture.
- If you prefer, you can grill the salmon patties instead of pan-frying them.
- Customize the dill aioli by adjusting the amount of garlic, dill, lemon juice, or seasoning to suit your taste.
- These salmon burgers can also be served without buns for a low-carb option, wrapped in lettuce leaves instead.

These salmon burgers with dill aioli are a wonderful way to enjoy salmon in a burger form. They're flavorful, moist, and perfect for a casual meal or outdoor barbecue. Give them a try for a tasty and satisfying dish!

Ceviche with Fresh Local Fish

Ingredients:

- 1 pound fresh local fish (such as snapper, sea bass, halibut, or tilapia), cut into small cubes
- 4-5 limes, juiced (enough to cover the fish)
- 1 small red onion, thinly sliced
- 1-2 tomatoes, diced
- 1 cucumber, peeled and diced
- 1 jalapeño or serrano pepper, seeded and minced (optional)
- 1/4 cup chopped fresh cilantro
- Salt and pepper, to taste
- Tortilla chips or tostadas, for serving

Instructions:

1. Prepare the Fish:
    - Rinse the fresh fish under cold water and pat it dry with paper towels. Cut the fish into small, bite-sized cubes and place them in a glass or ceramic bowl.
2. Marinate the Fish:
    - Squeeze enough fresh lime juice over the fish to completely cover it. The acidity of the lime juice will "cook" the fish. Make sure all the fish is submerged in the lime juice. Cover the bowl with plastic wrap and refrigerate for about 30 minutes to 1 hour. The fish should turn opaque and firm when ready.
3. Prepare the Vegetables:
    - While the fish is marinating, prepare the vegetables. Thinly slice the red onion, dice the tomatoes and cucumber, and mince the jalapeño or serrano pepper (if using). Place them in a large mixing bowl.
4. Assemble the Ceviche:
    - After the fish has marinated and "cooked" in the lime juice, drain off most of the lime juice from the fish (you can save a little for added flavor).
    - Add the marinated fish to the bowl with the vegetables.
    - Add chopped cilantro, salt, and pepper to taste. Gently toss everything together until well combined.
5. Chill and Serve:
    - Cover the ceviche mixture with plastic wrap and refrigerate for another 15-30 minutes to allow the flavors to meld together.

- Before serving, taste and adjust seasoning as needed with more salt, pepper, or lime juice.
- Serve the ceviche cold as an appetizer or light meal, accompanied by tortilla chips or tostadas for scooping.

Tips:

- Use the freshest fish available for the best results. Firm white fish works well for ceviche.
- Feel free to customize the ceviche with additional ingredients such as avocado slices, mango cubes, or grilled corn for added texture and flavor.
- Adjust the amount of jalapeño or serrano pepper according to your spice preference.
- Serve the ceviche immediately after chilling for the freshest taste and texture.

Ceviche with fresh local fish is a wonderful dish to enjoy during warm weather or as a light and refreshing appetizer any time of the year. The combination of citrus-marinated fish with crisp vegetables creates a vibrant and flavorful experience. Enjoy this traditional Latin American dish with family and friends!

Spicy Tuna Roll Sushi Bowl

Ingredients:

For the Spicy Tuna:

- 8 oz sushi-grade tuna, finely diced
- 2 tablespoons mayonnaise
- 1 tablespoon sriracha sauce (adjust to taste)
- 1 teaspoon soy sauce
- 1 teaspoon sesame oil
- 1 green onion, finely chopped
- 1/2 teaspoon sesame seeds (black or white), for garnish

For the Sushi Bowl:

- 2 cups cooked sushi rice, cooled
- 1 cucumber, julienned or sliced
- 1 avocado, sliced
- 1/4 cup sliced radishes
- 1/4 cup shredded nori (seaweed)
- Pickled ginger, for serving
- Wasabi, for serving
- Soy sauce, for serving

Instructions:

1. Prepare the Spicy Tuna:
    - In a mixing bowl, combine the finely diced tuna, mayonnaise, sriracha sauce, soy sauce, sesame oil, and chopped green onion. Mix well until the tuna is evenly coated with the spicy mayo sauce. Adjust the amount of sriracha sauce according to your spice preference.
2. Assemble the Sushi Bowl:
    - Divide the cooked sushi rice into serving bowls.
    - Arrange the julienned cucumber, sliced avocado, sliced radishes, and shredded nori around the rice in the bowl.
    - Spoon the spicy tuna mixture over the center of the rice.
3. Garnish and Serve:
    - Sprinkle sesame seeds over the spicy tuna.

- Serve the sushi bowl with pickled ginger, wasabi, and soy sauce on the side.
- Optionally, garnish with additional chopped green onions or extra sesame seeds for more flavor and texture.

4. Enjoy:
    - Use chopsticks or a fork to mix the ingredients together before eating, ensuring each bite has a combination of rice, vegetables, and spicy tuna.
    - Dip bites into soy sauce, wasabi, or pickled ginger for added flavor.

Tips:

- Use high-quality sushi-grade tuna for the best taste and texture in the spicy tuna mixture.
- Customize the sushi bowl with your favorite sushi ingredients such as tobiko (flying fish roe), edamame, or sliced seaweed salad.
- Adjust the level of spiciness by adding more or less sriracha sauce to the spicy tuna mixture.
- Feel free to substitute or add other vegetables such as sliced carrots, edamame beans, or cherry tomatoes based on your preference.
- Prepare the components ahead of time and assemble the sushi bowl just before serving for a quick and easy meal.

This Spicy Tuna Roll Sushi Bowl is a fun and delicious way to enjoy sushi flavors without the need for rolling sushi rolls. It's perfect for a light lunch or dinner and can be customized with your favorite sushi ingredients. Enjoy the bold and refreshing flavors of this sushi-inspired bowl!

Coconut Lime Shrimp Skewers

Ingredients:

- 1 pound large shrimp, peeled and deveined
- Zest and juice of 2 limes
- 3 tablespoons coconut milk
- 2 tablespoons soy sauce
- 2 tablespoons honey
- 2 cloves garlic, minced
- 1 teaspoon ground cumin
- 1/2 teaspoon ground coriander
- 1/2 teaspoon paprika
- Salt and pepper, to taste
- Wooden or metal skewers, soaked in water if using wooden ones
- Chopped fresh cilantro, for garnish
- Lime wedges, for serving

Instructions:

1. Prepare the Marinade:
    - In a bowl, combine the lime zest, lime juice, coconut milk, soy sauce, honey, minced garlic, ground cumin, ground coriander, paprika, salt, and pepper. Whisk together until well combined.
2. Marinate the Shrimp:
    - Place the peeled and deveined shrimp in a shallow dish or resealable plastic bag.
    - Pour the marinade over the shrimp, making sure they are well coated. Cover the dish or seal the bag, then refrigerate for at least 30 minutes to marinate. You can marinate longer for more flavor, up to 2 hours.
3. Skewer the Shrimp:
    - Preheat the grill or grill pan over medium-high heat.
    - Thread the marinated shrimp onto skewers, evenly dividing them among the skewers.
4. Grill the Shrimp:
    - Lightly oil the grill grates or grill pan to prevent sticking.
    - Place the shrimp skewers on the preheated grill or grill pan.
    - Grill the shrimp for 2-3 minutes per side, or until they turn pink and opaque. Be careful not to overcook the shrimp, as they can become rubbery.

5. Serve:
    - Remove the shrimp skewers from the grill and transfer them to a serving platter.
    - Garnish with chopped fresh cilantro and serve with lime wedges on the side for squeezing over the shrimp.

Tips:

- Use fresh or frozen shrimp for this recipe. If using frozen shrimp, thaw them completely before marinating.
- Adjust the amount of honey and lime juice based on your preference for sweetness and acidity.
- For a spicier version, add a pinch of red pepper flakes or finely chopped chili peppers to the marinade.
- Serve the coconut lime shrimp skewers as an appetizer or main dish, accompanied by rice or a fresh salad.
- These shrimp skewers can also be cooked on a broiler pan in the oven if you don't have a grill or grill pan.

Enjoy these delicious coconut lime shrimp skewers with their tropical flavors and vibrant colors. They make a wonderful addition to any summer barbecue or weeknight dinner!

Fish Tacos with Mango Salsa

Ingredients:

For the Fish Tacos:

- 1 pound white fish fillets (such as cod, tilapia, or mahi-mahi)
- 1 teaspoon ground cumin
- 1 teaspoon chili powder
- Salt and pepper, to taste
- 2 tablespoons olive oil
- 8 small corn or flour tortillas
- Shredded cabbage or lettuce, for serving
- Lime wedges, for serving

For the Mango Salsa:

- 1 ripe mango, peeled, pitted, and diced
- 1/2 red bell pepper, diced
- 1/4 cup finely chopped red onion
- 1 jalapeño pepper, seeded and minced
- Juice of 1 lime
- 2 tablespoons chopped fresh cilantro
- Salt and pepper, to taste

For the Creamy Lime Sauce (optional):

- 1/2 cup sour cream or Greek yogurt
- Juice of 1 lime
- 1-2 tablespoons chopped fresh cilantro
- Salt and pepper, to taste

Instructions:

1. Prepare the Mango Salsa:
    - In a bowl, combine the diced mango, diced red bell pepper, finely chopped red onion, minced jalapeño pepper, lime juice, chopped cilantro, salt, and pepper. Mix well to combine. Taste and adjust seasoning as needed. Set aside.

2. Prepare the Creamy Lime Sauce (optional):
   - In a separate bowl, whisk together the sour cream or Greek yogurt, lime juice, chopped cilantro, salt, and pepper to make the creamy lime sauce. Set aside.
3. Prepare the Fish:
   - Pat the fish fillets dry with paper towels.
   - In a small bowl, mix together the ground cumin, chili powder, salt, and pepper.
   - Rub the spice mixture evenly over both sides of the fish fillets.
4. Cook the Fish:
   - Heat the olive oil in a large skillet over medium-high heat.
   - Add the seasoned fish fillets to the skillet and cook for 3-4 minutes per side, or until the fish is cooked through and flakes easily with a fork. Cooking time will vary depending on the thickness of the fish.
5. Assemble the Tacos:
   - Warm the tortillas in a dry skillet or microwave.
   - To assemble each taco, place a portion of shredded cabbage or lettuce on a tortilla.
   - Top with a cooked fish fillet.
   - Spoon mango salsa over the fish.
   - Drizzle with creamy lime sauce, if desired.
   - Serve with lime wedges on the side.
6. Serve and Enjoy:
   - Serve the fish tacos immediately, garnished with extra chopped cilantro if desired.
   - Enjoy these delicious fish tacos with mango salsa for a burst of tropical flavors!

Tips:

- Choose a firm and mild-tasting white fish for the tacos, such as cod, tilapia, or mahi-mahi.
- Adjust the level of spiciness by adding more or less jalapeño pepper to the mango salsa.
- Customize the toppings by adding sliced avocado, diced tomatoes, or thinly sliced red onion to the tacos.
- Serve the fish tacos with rice and beans or a side salad for a complete meal.

These fish tacos with mango salsa are perfect for a casual dinner or summer gathering. They're light, flavorful, and guaranteed to be a hit with family and friends. Enjoy the combination of crispy fish and sweet-tangy mango salsa in each bite!

Smoked Trout Pâté with Crostini

Ingredients:

For the Smoked Trout Pâté:

- 8 oz smoked trout fillets, skin removed
- 4 oz cream cheese, softened
- 2 tablespoons mayonnaise
- 1 tablespoon lemon juice
- 1 tablespoon chopped fresh dill
- 1 tablespoon chopped chives (optional)
- Salt and pepper, to taste

For the Crostini:

- Baguette or crusty bread, sliced
- Olive oil
- Salt and pepper, to taste
- Fresh parsley or chives, chopped (for garnish)

Instructions:

1. Prepare the Smoked Trout Pâté:
    - In a food processor, combine the smoked trout fillets (skin removed), softened cream cheese, mayonnaise, lemon juice, chopped fresh dill, chopped chives (if using), salt, and pepper.
    - Pulse the mixture until smooth and well combined, scraping down the sides of the food processor as needed. Taste and adjust seasoning if necessary. Add more lemon juice, dill, or salt and pepper to taste.
2. Prepare the Crostini:
    - Preheat the oven to 375°F (190°C).
    - Slice the baguette or crusty bread into thin slices.
    - Arrange the bread slices on a baking sheet in a single layer.
    - Brush each slice of bread lightly with olive oil and sprinkle with salt and pepper.
3. Bake the Crostini:

- Place the baking sheet in the preheated oven and bake for 8-10 minutes, or until the crostini are golden brown and crispy. Keep an eye on them to prevent burning.
4. Assemble and Serve:
    - Once the crostini are ready, remove them from the oven and let them cool slightly.
    - Spread a generous amount of the smoked trout pâté onto each crostini.
    - Garnish with chopped fresh parsley or chives for added freshness and color.
5. Enjoy:
    - Arrange the smoked trout pâté crostini on a serving platter.
    - Serve the crostini as an appetizer or snack at your next gathering or party.
    - Enjoy the creamy and flavorful smoked trout pâté spread on crispy crostini!

Tips:

- Use high-quality smoked trout for the best flavor in the pâté.
- If you don't have a food processor, you can finely chop the smoked trout and mix it with the other ingredients using a fork or whisk.
- Customize the pâté by adding a touch of horseradish, Dijon mustard, or capers for additional flavor.
- Make the crostini and pâté ahead of time and assemble just before serving to save time during your event or gathering.

This smoked trout pâté with crostini is sure to impress your guests with its elegant presentation and delicious flavor. Enjoy this appetizer at your next party or as a special treat for yourself!

Fisherman's Stew with Seasonal Seafood

Ingredients:

- 1 pound mixed seasonal seafood (examples include shrimp, scallops, mussels, clams, firm fish such as cod or halibut), cleaned and prepared
- 1 onion, finely chopped
- 2 cloves garlic, minced
- 1 bell pepper (red, yellow, or orange), chopped
- 2 celery stalks, chopped
- 1 carrot, chopped
- 1 can (14 oz) diced tomatoes
- 4 cups seafood or fish stock
- 1/2 cup dry white wine (optional)
- 2 bay leaves
- 1 teaspoon dried thyme
- Salt and pepper, to taste
- Pinch of red pepper flakes (optional)
- Chopped fresh parsley or cilantro, for garnish
- Crusty bread, for serving

Instructions:

1. Prepare the Vegetables:
    - In a large pot or Dutch oven, heat a tablespoon of olive oil over medium heat.
    - Add the chopped onion, garlic, bell pepper, celery, and carrot to the pot.
    - Sauté for 5-7 minutes, or until the vegetables are softened and aromatic.
2. Add Tomatoes and Seasonings:
    - Stir in the diced tomatoes, seafood or fish stock, and white wine (if using).
    - Add the bay leaves, dried thyme, salt, pepper, and red pepper flakes (if using).
    - Bring the mixture to a simmer and cook for about 10 minutes to allow the flavors to meld together.
3. Add the Seafood:
    - Add the mixed seasonal seafood to the pot. Start with the seafood that takes longer to cook (such as firm fish), then add shrimp, scallops, mussels, and clams.

- Cover the pot and cook for 5-8 minutes, or until the seafood is cooked through and the mussels and clams have opened (discard any that do not open).
4. Serve:
    - Remove the pot from the heat.
    - Taste and adjust seasoning if needed with more salt, pepper, or red pepper flakes.
    - Ladle the fisherman's stew into bowls.
    - Garnish with chopped fresh parsley or cilantro.
    - Serve hot with crusty bread for dipping.

Tips:

- Use a variety of seafood that is fresh and in season. Adjust the cooking time for each type of seafood to ensure they are cooked perfectly.
- Feel free to add other vegetables such as potatoes or fennel to the stew for extra heartiness.
- For extra depth of flavor, you can use homemade seafood or fish stock. Otherwise, store-bought stock works well too.
- Serve the fisherman's stew as a main course with a side salad or enjoy it as a starter for a seafood-themed meal.

This fisherman's stew with seasonal seafood is a comforting and satisfying dish that highlights the natural flavors of the sea. It's perfect for a cozy dinner at home or for entertaining guests with a taste of the ocean. Enjoy this hearty and delicious stew with your favorite crusty bread!

Grilled Sardines with Lemon and Garlic

Ingredients:

- 8 fresh sardine fillets, cleaned and gutted
- 3 cloves garlic, minced
- Zest and juice of 1 lemon
- 3 tablespoons olive oil
- Salt and pepper, to taste
- Fresh parsley, chopped (for garnish)
- Lemon wedges, for serving

Instructions:

1. Prepare the Sardines:
    - Rinse the sardine fillets under cold water and pat them dry with paper towels.
    - Use a sharp knife to make a few shallow slashes on each side of the sardine fillets. This will help the marinade penetrate and the fish to cook evenly.
2. Make the Marinade:
    - In a bowl, combine the minced garlic, lemon zest, lemon juice, olive oil, salt, and pepper. Mix well to create the marinade.
3. Marinate the Sardines:
    - Place the sardine fillets in a shallow dish or resealable plastic bag.
    - Pour the marinade over the sardines, ensuring they are evenly coated.
    - Cover the dish or seal the bag, then refrigerate for at least 30 minutes to marinate. You can marinate longer for more flavor, up to 2 hours.
4. Preheat the Grill:
    - Preheat an outdoor grill or grill pan over medium-high heat.
5. Grill the Sardines:
    - Remove the sardines from the marinade, allowing any excess marinade to drip off.
    - Place the sardines on the preheated grill and cook for 3-4 minutes per side, or until the fish is cooked through and nicely charred. Sardines cook quickly, so keep an eye on them to prevent overcooking.
6. Serve:
    - Transfer the grilled sardines to a serving platter.
    - Garnish with chopped fresh parsley and serve with lemon wedges on the side for squeezing over the fish.

Tips:

- Choose fresh sardines for the best flavor. You can ask your fishmonger to clean and gut them for you.
- If you prefer less garlic flavor, you can reduce the amount of minced garlic in the marinade.
- Serve the grilled sardines with a side salad, grilled vegetables, or crusty bread for a complete meal.
- Be careful when flipping the sardines on the grill, as they are delicate and can break apart easily.

Grilled sardines with lemon and garlic are a delightful dish that showcases the natural flavor of the fish. Enjoy this simple and healthy recipe for a taste of the Mediterranean!

Lobster Risotto with Asparagus

Ingredients:

- 2 lobster tails (about 8 oz each), thawed if frozen
- 1 cup Arborio rice
- 4 cups seafood or chicken broth (approx.)
- 1/2 cup dry white wine
- 1 small onion, finely chopped
- 2 cloves garlic, minced
- 1 bunch asparagus, trimmed and cut into bite-sized pieces
- 1/2 cup grated Parmesan cheese
- 2 tablespoons unsalted butter
- 2 tablespoons olive oil
- Salt and pepper, to taste
- Chopped fresh parsley, for garnish

Instructions:

1. Prepare the Lobster:
    - Fill a large pot with water and bring it to a boil.
    - Add the lobster tails and cook for about 5-7 minutes, until the shells are bright red and the meat is opaque and firm.
    - Remove the lobster tails from the water and let them cool slightly.
    - Once cooled, remove the meat from the shells and chop it into bite-sized pieces. Set aside.
2. Prepare the Risotto:
    - In a saucepan, heat the seafood or chicken broth over medium heat until simmering. Keep it warm on the stove.
    - In a separate large, deep skillet or saucepan, heat the olive oil and butter over medium heat.
    - Add the chopped onion and garlic to the skillet and sauté for 2-3 minutes until softened and translucent.
3. Cook the Rice:
    - Add the Arborio rice to the skillet with the onions and garlic. Stir to coat the rice with the oil and butter.
    - Pour in the white wine and stir continuously until the wine is absorbed by the rice.
4. Add the Broth:

- Begin adding the warm broth to the skillet, one ladleful at a time, stirring frequently.
- Allow each ladleful of broth to be absorbed by the rice before adding the next. This process will take about 18-20 minutes until the rice is creamy and cooked al dente.
5. Add the Asparagus and Lobster:
    - About halfway through cooking the rice, add the chopped asparagus to the skillet.
    - Continue adding the broth and stirring until the rce is almost cooked.
    - Stir in the chopped lobster meat during the last few minutes of cooking, just to warm it through.
6. Finish and Serve:
    - Once the rice is creamy and cooked to your desired consistency, remove the skillet from the heat.
    - Stir in the grated Parmesan cheese and season with salt and pepper to taste.
    - Garnish the lobster risotto with chopped fresh parsley.
    - Serve immediately, while hot, in individual bowls or plates.

Tips:

- Use fresh lobster tails for the best flavor. If fresh lobster is not available, frozen lobster tails will also work.
- Risotto requires constant stirring to achieve a creamy texture. Be patient and enjoy the process!
- Adjust the amount of broth and cooking time as needed to reach the desired consistency of the risotto.
- Serve lobster risotto with a side salad or crusty bread for a complete meal.

This lobster risotto with asparagus is a sophisticated dish that is sure to impress. Enjoy the creamy texture of the risotto paired with the sweet and tender lobster meat and bright asparagus flavors. It's perfect for a romantic dinner or a special celebration!

Lemon Herb Baked Rainbow Trout

Ingredients:

- 4 rainbow trout fillets, about 6-8 ounces each
- 2 tablespoons olive oil
- 2 tablespoons fresh lemon juice
- Zest of 1 lemon
- 2 cloves garlic, minced
- 2 tablespoons chopped fresh parsley
- 1 tablespoon chopped fresh dill (or substitute with thyme or rosemary)
- Salt and pepper, to taste
- Lemon wedges, for serving
- Fresh herbs, for garnish (optional)

Instructions:

1. Preheat the Oven:
    - Preheat your oven to 400°F (200°C) and lightly grease a baking dish with olive oil or cooking spray.
2. Prepare the Trout Fillets:
    - Pat the rainbow trout fillets dry with paper towels.
    - Place the fillets skin-side down in the prepared baking dish.
3. Make the Lemon Herb Marinade:
    - In a small bowl, whisk together the olive oil, fresh lemon juice, lemon zest, minced garlic, chopped parsley, chopped dill, salt, and pepper.
4. Marinate the Trout:
    - Pour the lemon herb marinade over the rainbow trout fillets, making sure to coat them evenly on all sides.
    - Allow the trout to marinate for about 15-20 minutes at room temperature, or you can marinate in the refrigerator for up to 1 hour for more flavor.
5. Bake the Trout:
    - Place the baking dish with the marinated trout fillets in the preheated oven.
    - Bake for 12-15 minutes, depending on the thickness of the fillets, or until the trout is cooked through and flakes easily with a fork. The internal temperature of the trout should reach 145°F (63°C).
6. Serve:
    - Remove the baked rainbow trout from the oven.
    - Garnish with additional fresh herbs if desired.

- Serve the lemon herb baked rainbow trout immediately with lemon wedges on the side for squeezing over the fish.

Tips:

- Choose fresh rainbow trout fillets that are firm, moist, and have a mild aroma.
- Feel free to adjust the amount of garlic, lemon juice, or herbs according to your taste preferences.
- Serve the baked trout with a side of steamed vegetables, rice, or a green salad for a complete meal.
- Leftover baked trout can be stored in an airtight container in the refrigerator for up to 2 days. Enjoy it cold or gently reheated.

This lemon herb baked rainbow trout is a light and delicious dish that's perfect for seafood lovers. The combination of fresh herbs and zesty lemon complements the delicate flavor of the trout beautifully. Enjoy this recipe for a healthy and satisfying meal!

Tuna Nicoise Salad

Ingredients:

For the Salad:

- 1 pound baby potatoes (such as fingerling or new potatoes)
- 8 ounces green beans, trimmed
- 4 eggs
- 2 (5-ounce) cans of tuna in olive oil, drained
- 1 cup cherry tomatoes, halved
- 1/2 cup Niçoise olives (or substitute with Kalamata olives)
- 4 cups mixed salad greens (such as arugula or mesclun)
- Salt and pepper, to taste

For the Vinaigrette:

- 1/4 cup extra-virgin olive oil
- 2 tablespoons red wine vinegar
- 1 tablespoon Dijon mustard
- 1 garlic clove, minced
- 1 tablespoon chopped fresh parsley
- Salt and pepper, to taste

Optional Garnish:

- Anchovy fillets (optional)

Instructions:

1. Cook the Potatoes:
   - Place the baby potatoes in a pot of salted water. Bring to a boil, then reduce the heat and simmer for about 15-20 minutes, or until the potatoes are tender when pierced with a fork. Drain and let cool slightly.
2. Cook the Green Beans and Eggs:
   - While the potatoes are cooking, prepare a bowl of ice water. Bring another pot of salted water to a boil.
   - Add the green beans to the boiling water and cook for 3-4 minutes, until crisp-tender. Remove the green beans with a slotted spoon and

- immediately transfer them to the bowl of ice water to stop the cooking process.
        - In the same boiling water, carefully add the eggs and cook for 8-10 minutes for hard-boiled eggs. Transfer the eggs to the ice water bath to cool. Once cooled, peel the eggs and halve them.
    3. Prepare the Vinaigrette:
        - In a small bowl, whisk together the olive oil, red wine vinegar, Dijon mustard, minced garlic, chopped parsley, salt, and pepper until well combined. Set aside.
    4. Assemble the Salad:
        - Arrange the mixed salad greens on a large serving platter or individual plates.
        - Cut the cooked and cooled potatoes into halves or quarters and scatter them over the greens.
        - Arrange the blanched green beans, halved cherry tomatoes, drained tuna, hard-boiled eggs, and Niçoise olives on top of the salad.
    5. Serve the Salad:
        - Drizzle the vinaigrette over the salad just before serving.
        - Optionally, garnish the salad with anchovy fillets for extra flavor.
        - Season the salad with additional salt and pepper, if desired.

Tips:

- You can customize this salad by adding other ingredients such as red onion slices, capers, or cooked artichoke hearts.
- To save time, you can use canned or jarred green beans instead of blanching fresh green beans.
- Serve the Tuna Niçoise Salad with crusty bread or baguette slices for a complete and satisfying meal.

This Tuna Niçoise Salad is a wonderful choice for lunch or dinner, especially during warmer months. It's a well-balanced and delicious salad that celebrates the flavors of the Mediterranean. Enjoy this classic French salad with family and friends!

Clam Linguine with White Wine Sauce

Ingredients:

- 1 pound linguine pasta
- 2 pounds fresh clams (such as littleneck or Manila clams), scrubbed and cleaned
- 4 tablespoons unsalted butter
- 4 tablespoons olive oil
- 4 cloves garlic, minced
- 1/2 teaspoon red pepper flakes (adjust to taste)
- 1 cup dry white wine (such as Sauvignon Blanc or Pinot Grigio)
- 1/2 cup chopped fresh parsley
- Salt and pepper, to taste
- Grated Parmesan cheese, for serving (optional)
- Lemon wedges, for serving

Instructions:

1. Prepare the Clams:
    - Rinse the clams under cold water and scrub them to remove any dirt or sand. Discard any clams that are open and do not close when tapped, as they may be dead and should not be eaten.
2. Cook the Linguine:
    - Bring a large pot of salted water to a boil.
    - Add the linguine pasta and cook according to the package instructions until al dente.
    - Drain the pasta, reserving about 1 cup of the pasta cooking water.
3. Make the White Wine Sauce:
    - In a large skillet or saucepan, heat the butter and olive oil over medium heat.
    - Add the minced garlic and red pepper flakes to the pan. Cook for 1-2 minutes until the garlic becomes fragrant, but be careful not to let it brown.
4. Cook the Clams:
    - Increase the heat to medium-high.
    - Add the cleaned clams to the skillet.
    - Pour in the dry white wine and cover the skillet with a lid.
    - Cook for 5-7 minutes, shaking the pan occasionally, until the clams have opened.
    - Discard any clams that do not open.

5. Assemble the Dish:
    - Add the cooked linguine to the skillet with the clams and sauce.
    - Toss everything together gently, allowing the pasta to absorb the flavors of the sauce.
    - If the sauce seems too dry, add some of the reserved pasta cooking water to loosen it up.
    - Season with salt and pepper to taste.
6. Serve:
    - Transfer the clam linguine to serving plates or a large serving bowl.
    - Sprinkle with chopped fresh parsley.
    - Serve immediately, with grated Parmesan cheese on the side if desired.
    - Provide lemon wedges for squeezing over the pasta just before eating.

Tips:

- Choose fresh, high-quality clams for the best flavor. Discard any clams with broken shells or that do not close when tapped.
- If you prefer a thicker sauce, you can add a tablespoon or two of heavy cream to the sauce before tossing with the pasta.
- Serve the clam linguine with crusty bread or a side salad for a complete meal.
- Enjoy this dish with a glass of chilled white wine for a perfect pairing.

This clam linguine with white wine sauce is a delightful and elegant pasta dish that showcases the natural flavors of fresh seafood. It's perfect for a special dinner at home or for entertaining guests. Buon appetito!

Seared Sea Bass with Herb Butter

Ingredients:

- 4 sea bass fillets, skin-on, about 6-8 ounces each
- Salt and pepper, to taste
- 2 tablespoons olive oil
- 4 tablespoons unsalted butter, at room temperature
- 2 tablespoons chopped fresh parsley
- 1 tablespoon chopped fresh dill
- 1 tablespoon chopped fresh chives (or green onions)
- 2 cloves garlic, minced
- 1 tablespoon lemon juice
- Lemon wedges, for serving

Instructions:

1. Prepare the Herb Butter:
    - In a small bowl, combine the softened butter, chopped parsley, chopped dill, chopped chives (or green onions), minced garlic, and lemon juice.
    - Mix well until all ingredients are incorporated. Set aside.
2. Season and Prepare the Sea Bass:
    - Pat the sea bass fillets dry with paper towels.
    - Season both sides of the fillets generously with salt and pepper.
3. Heat the Skillet:
    - In a large skillet, heat the olive oil over medium-high heat until shimmering but not smoking.
4. Sear the Sea Bass:
    - Place the sea bass fillets in the skillet, skin-side down.
    - Cook undisturbed for about 4-5 minutes, or until the skin is crispy and golden brown.
    - Carefully flip the fillets using a spatula and cook for an additional 3-4 minutes, or until the fish is cooked through and flakes easily with a fork.
5. Add the Herb Butter:
    - Reduce the heat to low.
    - Add a tablespoon of the prepared herb butter to the skillet, allowing it to melt and coat the fish.
    - Spoon the melted herb butter over the sea bass fillets while they finish cooking for an additional minute.
6. Serve:

- Transfer the seared sea bass fillets to serving plates.
- Drizzle any remaining herb butter from the skillet over the fillets.
- Serve immediately with lemon wedges on the side for squeezing over the fish.

Tips:

- Use fresh sea bass fillets for the best flavor and texture.
- Adjust the amount of salt and pepper to your taste.
- Feel free to substitute or add other fresh herbs such as tarragon, basil, or cilantro to the herb butter.
- Serve the seared sea bass with your favorite side dishes, such as roasted vegetables, rice, or a fresh salad.

This seared sea bass with herb butter is a delightful dish that is perfect for a special dinner or entertaining guests. Enjoy the tender and flavorful sea bass with the aromatic herb butter sauce for a memorable meal!

Grilled Mackerel with Roasted Vegetables

Ingredients:

For the Grilled Mackerel:

- 4 mackerel fillets
- 2 tablespoons olive oil
- Salt and pepper, to taste
- Lemon wedges, for serving

For the Roasted Vegetables:

- 2 bell peppers (red, yellow, or orange), sliced
- 1 large red onion, sliced
- 1 zucchini, sliced
- 1 eggplant, sliced
- 1 pint cherry tomatoes
- 4 cloves garlic, minced
- 3 tablespoons olive oil
- 1 tablespoon balsamic vinegar
- 1 teaspoon dried oregano
- Salt and pepper, to taste
- Fresh parsley, chopped (for garnish)

Instructions:

1. Prepare the Mackerel:
    - Preheat the grill to medium-high heat.
    - Pat the mackerel fillets dry with paper towels.
    - Brush the fillets with olive oil and season with salt and pepper.
2. Grill the Mackerel:
    - Place the mackerel fillets on the preheated grill, skin-side down.
    - Grill for about 4-5 minutes on each side, or until the fish is cooked through and easily flakes with a fork.
    - Remove from the grill and set aside.
3. Prepare the Roasted Vegetables:
    - Preheat the oven to 400°F (200°C).
    - In a large mixing bowl, combine the sliced bell peppers, red onion, zucchini, eggplant, cherry tomatoes, minced garlic, olive oil, balsamic

vinegar, dried oregano, salt, and pepper. Toss until the vegetables are evenly coated.
4. Roast the Vegetables:
    - Spread the seasoned vegetables in a single layer on a baking sheet.
    - Roast in the preheated oven for 25-30 minutes, stirring halfway through cooking, or until the vegetables are tender and caramelized.
5. Serve the Dish:
    - Arrange the grilled mackerel fillets on a serving platter.
    - Spoon the roasted vegetables around the mackerel.
    - Garnish with chopped fresh parsley.
    - Serve immediately with lemon wedges on the side for squeezing over the fish.

Tips:

- Mackerel has a strong flavor that pairs well with the sweetness of roasted vegetables. However, you can substitute mackerel with other oily fish such as sardines or salmon.
- Feel free to use your favorite vegetables for roasting, such as carrots, broccoli, or cauliflower.
- Add extra flavor to the roasted vegetables by sprinkling them with grated Parmesan cheese before serving.
- Serve this dish with crusty bread or a side of couscous for a complete and satisfying meal.

This grilled mackerel with roasted vegetables is a delightful and nutritious dish that is perfect for any occasion. Enjoy the combination of tender fish and caramelized vegetables for a delicious and satisfying meal!

Stuffed Squid with Mediterranean Couscous

Ingredients:

For the Stuffed Squid:

- 8 small to medium-sized squid tubes, cleaned
- 1 cup couscous
- 1 1/4 cups chicken or vegetable broth
- 1/4 cup chopped sun-dried tomatoes (packed in oil), drained
- 1/4 cup chopped Kalamata olives
- 2 tablespoons chopped fresh parsley
- 2 tablespoons chopped fresh basil
- 2 tablespoons chopped fresh mint
- 2 cloves garlic, minced
- Zest and juice of 1 lemon
- 3 tablespoons olive oil
- Salt and pepper, to taste

For Cooking the Squid:

- 2 tablespoons olive oil
- Salt and pepper, to taste

For Serving:

- Lemon wedges
- Extra chopped fresh herbs (parsley, basil, mint) for garnish

Instructions:

1. Prepare the Couscous:
    - In a saucepan, bring the chicken or vegetable broth to a boil.
    - Stir in the couscous, cover the pan, and remove from heat. Let it sit for 5 minutes to allow the couscous to absorb the liquid.
    - Fluff the couscous with a fork and transfer it to a large mixing bowl to cool slightly.
2. Prepare the Stuffing Mixture:

- To the couscous, add the chopped sun-dried tomatoes, Kalamata olives, chopped parsley, basil, mint, minced garlic, lemon zest, lemon juice, and olive oil.
- Season the mixture with salt and pepper to taste. Stir well to combine all ingredients.
3. Stuff the Squid:
    - Preheat the oven to 375°F (190°C).
    - Rinse the squid tubes under cold water and pat them dry with paper towels.
    - Using a spoon, carefully stuff each squid tube with the couscous mixture, leaving some room at the top to secure the opening with a toothpick.
4. Cook the Stuffed Squid:
    - Heat 2 tablespoons of olive oil in an oven-safe skillet or baking dish over medium-high heat.
    - Season the stuffed squid with salt and pepper.
    - Sear the squid tubes in the hot skillet for about 2-3 minutes on each side until lightly browned.
5. Finish Cooking in the Oven:
    - Transfer the skillet or baking dish to the preheated oven.
    - Bake the stuffed squid for 15-20 minutes, or until the squid is cooked through and tender.
6. Serve:
    - Remove the toothpicks from the stuffed squid before serving.
    - Garnish with extra chopped fresh herbs and lemon wedges.
    - Serve the stuffed squid with Mediterranean couscous immediately as a main dish.

Tips:

- Choose squid tubes that are cleaned and ready to be stuffed.
- Feel free to adjust the stuffing ingredients based on your preferences. You can add pine nuts, capers, or diced tomatoes to the couscous mixture for additional flavor.
- Be careful not to overcook the squid, as it can become tough. The squid is done when it turns opaque and can be easily pierced with a fork.
- Serve this dish with a side salad or steamed vegetables for a complete and satisfying meal.

This stuffed squid with Mediterranean couscous is a delightful and impressive dish that's perfect for a special dinner or entertaining guests. Enjoy the combination of tender squid and flavorful couscous for a taste of the Mediterranean!

Salmon Teriyaki Skewers

Ingredients:

- 1 pound salmon fillets, skinless, cut into cubes
- Wooden or metal skewers (if using wooden skewers, soak them in water for 30 minutes before grilling)

For the Teriyaki Marinade:

- 1/3 cup soy sauce
- 1/4 cup mirin (Japanese sweet rice wine)
- 2 tablespoons honey or brown sugar
- 2 tablespoons rice vinegar
- 2 cloves garlic, minced
- 1 tablespoon grated fresh ginger
- 1 tablespoon sesame oil
- 2 green onions, chopped (for garnish)
- Sesame seeds, for garnish (optional)

Instructions:

1. Prepare the Salmon:
    - Cut the salmon fillets into bite-sized cubes.
    - Thread the salmon pieces onto skewers, leaving a little space between each piece for even cooking.
2. Make the Teriyaki Marinade:
    - In a small saucepan, combine the soy sauce, mirin, honey or brown sugar, rice vinegar, minced garlic, grated ginger, and sesame oil.
    - Heat the mixture over medium heat, stirring frequently, until the sugar is dissolved and the sauce slightly thickens (about 5-7 minutes). Remove from heat and let it cool.
3. Marinate the Salmon Skewers:
    - Reserve about 1/4 cup of the teriyaki marinade for basting later.
    - Pour the remaining marinade over the salmon skewers, ensuring all pieces are coated.
    - Cover and refrigerate for at least 30 minutes to allow the flavors to penetrate the salmon.
4. Preheat the Grill:

- Preheat your grill to medium-high heat. Make sure the grates are clean and lightly oiled to prevent sticking.

5. Grill the Salmon Skewers:
    - Remove the salmon skewers from the marinade (discard the used marinade).
    - Place the skewers on the preheated grill and cook for about 3-4 minutes per side, or until the salmon is cooked through and has grill marks.
    - While grilling, brush the reserved teriyaki marinade onto the salmon skewers for extra flavor.
6. Serve the Salmon Teriyaki Skewers:
    - Transfer the grilled salmon skewers to a serving platter.
    - Garnish with chopped green onions and sesame seeds (if using).
    - Serve immediately with steamed rice and your favorite vegetables.

Tips:

- If you prefer, you can broil the salmon skewers in the oven instead of grilling. Preheat the broiler, place the skewers on a foil-lined baking sheet, and broil for about 4-5 minutes per side, basting with the teriyaki marinade.
- Make sure not to overcook the salmon to keep it tender and juicy.
- Customize the teriyaki marinade by adjusting the sweetness (add more honey or sugar) or adding a touch of heat with red pepper flakes or Sriracha sauce.
- Serve leftover teriyaki sauce on the side for dipping.

Enjoy these delicious salmon teriyaki skewers as a tasty and satisfying meal that's bursting with Asian-inspired flavors!

Scallop and Corn Chowder

Ingredients:

- 1 pound fresh sea scallops, muscle removed
- 4 slices bacon, chopped
- 1 tablespoon butter
- 1 onion, finely chopped
- 2 cloves garlic, minced
- 2 celery stalks, diced
- 2 medium potatoes, peeled and diced
- 3 cups fresh or frozen corn kernels (about 4 ears of corn)
- 4 cups chicken or vegetable broth
- 1 cup heavy cream
- 1 bay leaf
- 1/2 teaspoon dried thyme
- Salt and pepper, to taste
- Chopped fresh parsley, for garnish

Instructions:

1. Prepare the Scallops:
    - Pat the scallops dry with paper towels and season them lightly with salt and pepper. Set aside.
2. Cook the Bacon:
    - In a large soup pot or Dutch oven, cook the chopped bacon over medium heat until crispy.
    - Remove the cooked bacon with a slotted spoon and set aside on a paper towel-lined plate.
3. Sauté the Vegetables:
    - Add the butter to the bacon fat in the pot. Once melted, add the chopped onion, minced garlic, and diced celery.
    - Sauté for 3-4 minutes until the vegetables start to soften.
4. Add Potatoes and Corn:
    - Stir in the diced potatoes and corn kernels. Cook for another 3-4 minutes, stirring occasionally.
5. Simmer the Chowder:
    - Pour in the chicken or vegetable broth and add the bay leaf and dried thyme.

- Bring the mixture to a boil, then reduce the heat to low and let it simmer for about 15-20 minutes, or until the potatoes are tender.
6. Add the Scallops and Cream:
    - Stir in the heavy cream and cooked bacon.
    - Gently add the seasoned scallops to the pot and simmer for another 3-4 minutes, or until the scallops are opaque and cooked through. Be careful not to overcook the scallops.
7. Season and Serve:
    - Taste the chowder and season with salt and pepper as needed.
    - Remove the bay leaf before serving.
    - Ladle the scallop and corn chowder into bowls.
    - Garnish with chopped fresh parsley and serve hot.

Tips:

- Choose fresh, dry-packed scallops for the best flavor and texture.
- If using frozen corn, thaw it before adding to the chowder.
- For extra richness, you can stir in a couple of tablespoons of butter or grated Parmesan cheese at the end of cooking.
- Serve the scallop and corn chowder with crusty bread or oyster crackers for a complete meal.

This scallop and corn chowder is a comforting and satisfying soup that's perfect for any occasion. Enjoy the creamy texture, sweet corn, and tender scallops in every spoonful!

Baked Stuffed Shrimp with Herbed Crumbs

Ingredients:

- 12 large shrimp, peeled and deveined, tails left on
- 1 cup fresh breadcrumbs (from about 2-3 slices of bread)
- 2 tablespoons chopped fresh parsley
- 1 tablespoon chopped fresh chives (or green onions)
- 1 tablespoon chopped fresh dill
- 1 clove garlic, minced
- Zest of 1 lemon
- 2 tablespoons grated Parmesan cheese
- 3 tablespoons unsalted butter, melted
- Salt and pepper, to taste
- Lemon wedges, for serving
- Chopped fresh parsley, for garnish

Instructions:

1. Preheat the Oven:
    - Preheat your oven to 375°F (190°C). Lightly grease a baking dish with butter or olive oil.
2. Prepare the Shrimp:
    - Use a paring knife to make a deep slit along the back of each shrimp (where it was deveined), taking care not to cut all the way through.
    - Gently press open the shrimp to create a "butterfly" shape.
3. Make the Herbed Crumb Mixture:
    - In a mixing bowl, combine the fresh breadcrumbs, chopped parsley, chives, dill, minced garlic, lemon zest, grated Parmesan cheese, melted butter, salt, and pepper. Mix well to combine.
4. Stuff the Shrimp:
    - Spoon a generous amount of the herbed breadcrumb mixture into the slit of each shrimp, pressing gently to close the shrimp around the filling.
5. Arrange in Baking Dish:
    - Place the stuffed shrimp in a single layer in the prepared baking dish.
6. Bake the Stuffed Shrimp:
    - Bake the stuffed shrimp in the preheated oven for 12-15 minutes, or until the shrimp are cooked through and the breadcrumbs are golden and crispy.
7. Serve:

- Remove the baked stuffed shrimp from the oven.
- Garnish with chopped fresh parsley and serve immediately with lemon wedges on the side for squeezing over the shrimp.

Tips:

- Choose large shrimp for this recipe, as they are easier to stuff and make a more impressive presentation.
- You can use store-bought breadcrumbs or make your own by processing fresh bread slices in a food processor until finely crumbled.
- Customize the herb mixture by adding other herbs such as basil or tarragon, or a pinch of red pepper flakes for a spicy kick.
- Serve the baked stuffed shrimp as an appetizer or main course with a side salad or roasted vegetables.

This baked stuffed shrimp with herbed crumbs is a flavorful and elegant dish that's sure to impress your guests. Enjoy the delicious combination of tender shrimp and savory breadcrumb filling!

Shrimp and Vegetable Stir-Fry

Ingredients:

- 1 pound large shrimp, peeled and deveined
- 2 cups broccoli florets
- 1 red bell pepper, sliced
- 1 yellow bell pepper, sliced
- 1 carrot, sliced into thin strips
- 1 cup snow peas, trimmed
- 4 green onions, sliced
- 3 cloves garlic, minced
- 1-inch piece of ginger, grated
- 2 tablespoons soy sauce (low-sodium recommended)
- 2 tablespoons oyster sauce
- 1 tablespoon hoisin sauce
- 1 tablespoon rice vinegar
- 1 tablespoon sesame oil
- 2 tablespoons vegetable oil (for stir-frying)
- Cooked rice or noodles, for serving
- Sesame seeds and chopped fresh cilantro (optional), for garnish

Instructions:

1. Prepare the Shrimp:
    - Pat the shrimp dry with paper towels and season lightly with salt and pepper.
2. Make the Stir-Fry Sauce:
    - In a small bowl, whisk together the soy sauce, oyster sauce, hoisin sauce, rice vinegar, and sesame oil. Set aside.
3. Stir-Fry the Vegetables:
    - Heat 1 tablespoon of vegetable oil in a large skillet or wok over medium-high heat.
    - Add the minced garlic and grated ginger, and stir-fry for about 30 seconds until fragrant.
    - Add the broccoli florets, sliced bell peppers, carrot strips, and snow peas to the skillet. Stir-fry for 3-4 minutes until the vegetables are crisp-tender. Remove the vegetables from the skillet and set aside.
4. Cook the Shrimp:
    - Add another tablespoon of vegetable oil to the skillet.

- Add the seasoned shrimp to the skillet and stir-fry for 2-3 minutes until the shrimp turn pink and opaque.
5. Combine Everything:
    - Return the cooked vegetables to the skillet with the shrimp.
    - Pour the stir-fry sauce over the shrimp and vegetables. Toss everything together until well coated and heated through.
6. Serve:
    - Serve the shrimp and vegetable stir-fry immediately over cooked rice or noodles.
    - Garnish with sesame seeds and chopped fresh cilantro, if desired.

Tips:

- Use a variety of colorful vegetables for visual appeal and flavor. Feel free to customize with your favorites such as snap peas, baby corn, or water chestnuts.
- Make sure your skillet or wok is hot before adding ingredients for quick stir-frying.
- Don't overcook the shrimp to keep them tender and juicy.
- You can adjust the amount of sauce based on your preference. Add more soy sauce for saltiness or hoisin sauce for sweetness.
- Serve this dish as a complete meal or pair it with a side of steamed edamame or Asian-inspired slaw.

This shrimp and vegetable stir-fry is a versatile and satisfying meal that's perfect for busy weeknights. Enjoy the vibrant flavors and textures of this delicious stir-fry dish!

Lemon Garlic Butter Crab Legs

Ingredients:

- 2 pounds crab legs (snow crab or king crab)
- 1/2 cup unsalted butter
- 4 cloves garlic, minced
- Zest and juice of 1 lemon
- 2 tablespoons chopped fresh parsley
- Salt and black pepper, to taste
- Lemon wedges, for serving

Instructions:

1. Prepare the Crab Legs:
    - If using frozen crab legs, thaw them in the refrigerator overnight or according to package instructions. Rinse them under cold water to remove any ice crystals.
2. Preheat the Oven:
    - Preheat your oven to 400°F (200°C).
3. Prepare the Lemon Garlic Butter Sauce:
    - In a small saucepan, melt the butter over medium heat.
    - Add the minced garlic to the melted butter and cook for 1-2 minutes until fragrant.
    - Stir in the lemon zest and lemon juice. Season with salt and black pepper to taste.
    - Remove the saucepan from heat and stir in the chopped fresh parsley. Set aside.
4. Crack and Arrange the Crab Legs:
    - Use kitchen shears or a crab cracker to crack the crab legs slightly along the shell to help the butter sauce penetrate.
    - Arrange the crab legs in a single layer on a baking sheet or large oven-safe dish.
5. Pour the Lemon Garlic Butter Sauce:
    - Pour the prepared lemon garlic butter sauce evenly over the crab legs, making sure to coat them well.
6. Bake the Crab Legs:
    - Place the baking sheet or dish in the preheated oven.
    - Bake the crab legs for 10-12 minutes, or until heated through.
7. Serve the Lemon Garlic Butter Crab Legs:

- Remove the crab legs from the oven.
- Transfer the crab legs to a serving platter.
- Pour any remaining butter sauce from the baking sheet over the crab legs.
- Serve immediately with lemon wedges on the side for squeezing over the crab meat.

Tips:

- Choose either snow crab legs or king crab legs based on your preference and availability.
- Feel free to add additional herbs such as thyme or chives to the butter sauce for extra flavor.
- Serve the lemon garlic butter crab legs with crusty bread or a side salad for a complete meal.
- Provide seafood crackers and small forks for easy cracking and eating of the crab legs.

Enjoy these lemon garlic butter crab legs as a decadent and flavorful seafood dish that's perfect for any occasion. Savor the sweet and tender crab meat with the zesty and buttery sauce!

Grilled Mahi-Mahi Tacos with Pineapple Salsa

Ingredients:

For the Mahi-Mahi Tacos:

- 1 pound mahi-mahi fillets, skin removed
- 8 small flour or corn tortillas
- 2 tablespoons olive oil
- 1 teaspoon chili powder
- 1/2 teaspoon cumin
- Salt and pepper, to taste
- Shredded cabbage or lettuce, for serving
- Lime wedges, for serving

For the Pineapple Salsa:

- 1 cup diced fresh pineapple
- 1/2 cup diced red bell pepper
- 1/4 cup diced red onion
- 2 tablespoons chopped fresh cilantro
- Juice of 1 lime
- Salt and pepper, to taste

For the Chipotle Lime Crema (optional):

- 1/2 cup sour cream or Greek yogurt
- 1 tablespoon adobo sauce (from canned chipotle peppers)
- Juice of 1 lime
- Salt, to taste

Instructions:

1. Prepare the Mahi-Mahi:
    - Preheat your grill or grill pan over medium-high heat.
    - Pat the mahi-mahi fillets dry with paper towels.
    - In a small bowl, mix together the olive oil, chili powder, cumin, salt, and pepper.
    - Brush the seasoning mixture onto both sides of the mahi-mahi fillets.

2. Grill the Mahi-Mahi:
   - Place the seasoned mahi-mahi fillets on the preheated grill.
   - Grill for 3-4 minutes per side, or until the fish is cooked through and easily flakes with a fork.
   - Remove from the grill and let rest for a few minutes.
3. Make the Pineapple Salsa:
   - In a medium bowl, combine the diced pineapple, red bell pepper, red onion, chopped cilantro, lime juice, salt, and pepper.
   - Stir well to combine. Adjust seasoning to taste.
4. Prepare the Chipotle Lime Crema (optional):
   - In a small bowl, mix together the sour cream or Greek yogurt, adobo sauce, lime juice, and salt.
   - Stir until smooth and well combined. Adjust seasoning to taste.
5. Assemble the Tacos:
   - Heat the tortillas on the grill or in a skillet until warmed and slightly charred.
   - Flake the grilled mahi-mahi into chunks using a fork.
   - Place some shredded cabbage or lettuce on each tortilla.
   - Top with the flaked mahi-mahi and a generous spoonful of pineapple salsa.
   - Drizzle with chipotle lime crema, if using.
   - Serve the tacos immediately with lime wedges on the side.

Tips:

- You can substitute mahi-mahi with other firm white fish such as cod, snapper, or halibut for these tacos.
- Customize the salsa by adding diced jalapeño or mango for extra spice and sweetness.
- The chipotle lime crema adds a creamy and tangy kick to the tacos, but you can also use regular sour cream or skip the crema altogether.
- Serve these grilled mahi-mahi tacos with rice and beans or a side of Mexican street corn for a complete and delicious meal.

Enjoy these grilled mahi-mahi tacos with pineapple salsa for a taste of tropical paradise!

The combination of tender fish, sweet pineapple, and zesty flavors is sure to be a hit at your next taco night.

Coconut-Crusted Shrimp with Mango Dipping Sauce

Ingredients:

For the Coconut-Crusted Shrimp:

- 1 pound large shrimp, peeled and deveined, tails left on
- 1 cup sweetened shredded coconut
- 1/2 cup panko breadcrumbs (or regular breadcrumbs)
- 1/2 teaspoon salt
- 1/4 teaspoon black pepper
- 2 eggs
- 2 tablespoons all-purpose flour
- Vegetable oil, for frying

For the Mango Dipping Sauce:

- 1 ripe mango, peeled and diced
- 1/4 cup mayonnaise
- 2 tablespoons Greek yogurt (or sour cream)
- 1 tablespoon honey
- 1 tablespoon lime juice
- 1/4 teaspoon cayenne pepper (optional, for a spicy kick)
- Salt, to taste

For Serving:

- Lime wedges
- Chopped fresh cilantro or parsley, for garnish

Instructions:

1. Prepare the Mango Dipping Sauce:
    - In a blender or food processor, combine the diced mango, mayonnaise, Greek yogurt (or sour cream), honey, lime juice, and cayenne pepper (if using).
    - Blend until smooth and creamy.
    - Season with salt to taste. Transfer to a serving bowl and refrigerate until ready to use.

2. Prepare the Coconut-Crusted Shrimp:
   - In a shallow bowl, combine the sweetened shredded coconut, panko breadcrumbs, salt, and black pepper. Mix well.
   - In another shallow bowl, lightly beat the eggs.
   - Place the all-purpose flour in a third shallow bowl.
3. Coat and Fry the Shrimp:
   - Pat the shrimp dry with paper towels.
   - Dip each shrimp first into the flour, shaking off any excess.
   - Next, dip the shrimp into the beaten eggs, allowing any excess to drip off.
   - Finally, coat the shrimp with the coconut breadcrumb mixture, pressing gently to adhere the coating.
   - Heat vegetable oil in a large skillet or frying pan over medium-high heat.
   - Fry the coated shrimp in batches for about 2-3 minutes per side, or until golden brown and crispy.
   - Transfer the fried shrimp to a plate lined with paper towels to drain excess oil.
4. Serve the Coconut-Crusted Shrimp:
   - Arrange the coconut-crusted shrimp on a serving platter.
   - Garnish with chopped fresh cilantro or parsley.
   - Serve immediately with the mango dipping sauce and lime wedges on the side.

Tips:

- Use large shrimp for this recipe, as they are easier to coat and make a more substantial appetizer or main dish.
- Adjust the amount of cayenne pepper in the mango dipping sauce to control the level of spiciness.
- For a healthier option, you can bake the coconut-crusted shrimp in the oven instead of frying. Place the coated shrimp on a baking sheet lined with parchment paper and bake at 400°F (200°C) for 10-12 minutes, flipping halfway through.

Enjoy these crispy and flavorful coconut-crusted shrimp with mango dipping sauce as a crowd-pleasing appetizer or main course! The combination of sweet coconut and tangy mango is sure to impress your guests.

Tuna Steaks with Sesame Ginger Glaze

Ingredients:

For the Tuna Steaks:

- 4 tuna steaks (about 6-8 ounces each), fresh or thawed if frozen
- Salt and pepper, to taste
- 1 tablespoon vegetable oil (for searing)

For the Sesame Ginger Glaze:

- 1/4 cup soy sauce (low-sodium recommended)
- 2 tablespoons honey
- 2 tablespoons rice vinegar
- 1 tablespoon sesame oil
- 2 teaspoons freshly grated ginger
- 2 cloves garlic, minced
- 1 tablespoon sesame seeds, for garnish
- Thinly sliced green onions, for garnish

Instructions:

1. Prepare the Sesame Ginger Glaze:
    - In a small saucepan, combine the soy sauce, honey, rice vinegar, sesame oil, grated ginger, and minced garlic.
    - Heat the mixture over medium heat, stirring occasionally, until the sauce begins to simmer and slightly thickens (about 3-4 minutes).
    - Remove from heat and set aside.
2. Prepare the Tuna Steaks:
    - Pat the tuna steaks dry with paper towels and season both sides with salt and pepper.
    - Heat the vegetable oil in a large skillet or grill pan over medium-high heat.
3. Sear the Tuna Steaks:
    - Carefully place the tuna steaks in the hot skillet or grill pan.
    - Sear the tuna for about 2-3 minutes on each side (for rare to medium-rare), or adjust cooking time based on your preference and the thickness of the tuna steaks.
    - Remove the tuna steaks from the skillet and transfer to a plate. Tent loosely with foil and let rest for a few minutes.

4. Serve the Tuna Steaks:
    - Drizzle the sesame ginger glaze over the seared tuna steaks.
    - Sprinkle with sesame seeds and thinly sliced green onions for garnish.
    - Serve the tuna steaks immediately with your choice of side dishes, such as steamed rice, stir-fried vegetables, or a fresh salad.

Tips:

- Choose high-quality tuna steaks for the best flavor and texture. Look for fresh tuna steaks at your local seafood market or grocery store.
- Adjust the sweetness of the glaze by adding more or less honey to suit your taste.
- For a spicier glaze, add a pinch of red pepper flakes or a dash of sriracha sauce.
- Be cautious not to overcook the tuna steaks to keep them tender and moist. Aim for a nice sear on the outside while keeping the center pink and rare to medium-rare.
- If using a grill, preheat it to medium-high heat and lightly oil the grates before adding the tuna steaks.

Enjoy these delicious tuna steaks with sesame ginger glaze for a restaurant-quality meal at home! The combination of savory-sweet glaze and perfectly seared tuna is sure to impress your family and friends.

Smoked Haddock and Leek Gratin

Ingredients:

- 1 pound smoked haddock fillets (or smoked cod), skinless and boneless
- 2 large leeks, washed and sliced
- 3 tablespoons butter
- 3 tablespoons all-purpose flour
- 2 cups milk
- 1 cup grated Gruyère or cheddar cheese
- Salt and pepper, to taste
- 1/4 teaspoon nutmeg (optional)
- 1 cup fresh breadcrumbs
- 2 tablespoons chopped fresh parsley
- Lemon wedges, for serving

Instructions:

1. Prepare the Smoked Haddock:
    - Preheat your oven to 375°F (190°C).
    - Place the smoked haddock fillets in a shallow baking dish. Cover with cold water and let them soak for 10-15 minutes to reduce the smoky flavor slightly.
    - Drain the haddock and pat dry with paper towels. Cut the fish into large chunks and set aside.
2. Cook the Leeks:
    - In a large skillet, melt 2 tablespoons of butter over medium heat.
    - Add the sliced leeks to the skillet and sauté for 5-7 minutes, or until the leeks are softened and starting to caramelize. Remove from heat and set aside.
3. Make the Cheese Sauce:
    - In a saucepan, melt the remaining 1 tablespoon of butter over medium heat.
    - Stir in the all-purpose flour to make a roux. Cook for 1-2 minutes, stirring constantly.
    - Gradually whisk in the milk, stirring continuously to avoid lumps.
    - Cook the sauce until thickened and smooth, about 5-7 minutes.
    - Stir in the grated cheese until melted and well combined.
    - Season the sauce with salt, pepper, and nutmeg (if using).
4. Assemble the Gratin:

- Arrange the cooked leeks and smoked haddock chunks in a baking dish.
- Pour the cheese sauce evenly over the leeks and haddock.

5. Top with Breadcrumbs:
    - In a small bowl, combine the fresh breadcrumbs with chopped parsley.
    - Sprinkle the breadcrumb mixture evenly over the top of the gratin.
6. Bake the Gratin:
    - Place the baking dish in the preheated oven and bake for 25-30 minutes, or until the gratin is bubbling and the top is golden brown.
7. Serve the Gratin:
    - Remove the gratin from the oven and let it cool slightly before serving.
    - Garnish with additional chopped parsley, if desired.
    - Serve the smoked haddock and leek gratin with lemon wedges on the side for squeezing over the fish.

Tips:

- You can use other types of smoked fish such as smoked cod or smoked trout for this recipe.
- Feel free to add a handful of cooked, chopped spinach or peas to the gratin for added color and flavor.
- Serve this gratin as a main dish with a side salad and crusty bread, or as a side dish with roasted vegetables or mashed potatoes.

Enjoy this comforting and flavorful smoked haddock and leek gratin as a satisfying meal for lunch or dinner! The creamy cheese sauce and golden breadcrumb topping complement the smoky fish and sweet leeks perfectly.

Paella with Sustainable Seafood Mix

Ingredients:

- 1 pound mixed sustainable seafood (such as shrimp, mussels, clams, squid, and firm white fish like cod or halibut), cleaned and prepared
- 2 cups Spanish paella rice (such as Bomba rice or Arborio rice)
- 4 cups seafood or chicken broth
- 1 onion, finely chopped
- 4 cloves garlic, minced
- 1 red bell pepper, diced
- 1 green bell pepper, diced
- 1 cup fresh or frozen peas
- 1 tomato, diced
- 1 teaspoon smoked paprika
- 1/2 teaspoon saffron threads (or powdered saffron)
- 1 lemon, cut into wedges
- Salt and pepper, to taste
- Olive oil
- Chopped fresh parsley, for garnish

Instructions:

1. Prepare the Seafood:
    - Clean and prepare the seafood as needed. Peel and devein shrimp, scrub mussels and clams, and slice squid into rings. Season lightly with salt and pepper.
2. Make the Saffron Broth:
    - In a small saucepan, heat the seafood or chicken broth over low heat. Add the saffron threads and let steep for 5-10 minutes to infuse the broth with flavor and color. Keep warm.
3. Cook the Vegetables:
    - In a large paella pan or wide skillet, heat a few tablespoons of olive oil over medium heat.
    - Add the chopped onion and cook until softened, about 3-4 minutes.
    - Stir in the minced garlic and diced bell peppers. Cook for another 2-3 minutes until the vegetables start to soften.
4. Add Rice and Spices:
    - Add the Spanish paella rice to the pan, stirring to coat the rice in the olive oil and vegetables.

- Sprinkle in the smoked paprika and diced tomato. Stir to combine.
5. Cook the Paella:
    - Pour the warm saffron-infused broth over the rice and vegetables in the pan. Stir gently to distribute the ingredients evenly.
    - Bring the mixture to a simmer. Cook uncovered for about 10 minutes, gently stirring occasionally.
6. Arrange the Seafood:
    - Nestle the mixed seafood into the partially cooked rice mixture, distributing it evenly across the pan.
    - Arrange mussels and clams with the hinge side down, pushing them into the rice.
    - Scatter peas over the top of the paella.
7. Finish Cooking:
    - Continue to cook the paella uncovered for another 10-12 minutes, or until the rice is tender, the seafood is cooked through, and the liquid is absorbed.
    - If needed, cover the paella with foil during the last few minutes to help the seafood steam and open the shellfish.
8. Serve the Paella:
    - Remove the paella from the heat and let it rest for a few minutes.
    - Garnish with chopped fresh parsley and serve hot with lemon wedges on the side.

Tips:

- Use sustainably sourced seafood for this recipe to support responsible fishing practices.
- You can customize the seafood mix based on availability and preference. Include your favorite seafood like scallops, squid, or lobster.
- Don't stir the paella too much once the seafood is added to avoid breaking apart delicate seafood.
- Serve the paella directly from the pan for a beautiful presentation.
- Enjoy this delicious paella with a glass of Spanish wine for a complete and satisfying meal!

This paella with sustainable seafood mix is a festive and impressive dish that's perfect for gatherings or special occasions. The combination of flavors and textures will transport you to the shores of Spain!

Grilled Calamari Salad with Fennel and Orange

Ingredients:

- 4 large portobello mushrooms, stems removed and cleaned
- 1 tablespoon olive oil
- Salt and pepper, to taste
- 1 tablespoon butter
- 1 small onion, finely chopped
- 2 cloves garlic, minced
- 1 red bell pepper, finely chopped
- 1/2 cup breadcrumbs (preferably panko)
- 1 pound lump crabmeat, picked over for shells
- 1/4 cup mayonnaise
- 1 tablespoon Dijon mustard
- 1 tablespoon lemon juice
- 1/4 cup chopped fresh parsley
- 1/4 cup grated Parmesan cheese
- Lemon wedges, for serving
- Chopped fresh parsley or chives, for garnish

Instructions:

1. Prepare the Portobello Mushrooms:
    - Preheat your oven to 400°F (200°C).
    - Brush the portobello mushroom caps with olive oil and season them with salt and pepper.
    - Place the mushrooms on a baking sheet, gill side up. Bake for 10-12 minutes until slightly softened. Remove from the oven and set aside.
2. Make the Crab Stuffing:
    - In a skillet, melt the butter over medium heat.
    - Add the chopped onion and red bell pepper. Cook for 3-4 minutes until softened.
    - Stir in the minced garlic and cook for another 1-2 minutes until fragrant.
    - Remove the skillet from the heat and let the mixture cool slightly.
3. Prepare the Crab Filling:
    - In a large mixing bowl, combine the cooked onion and pepper mixture with breadcrumbs, lump crabmeat, mayonnaise, Dijon mustard, lemon juice, chopped parsley, and grated Parmesan cheese.
    - Mix until well combined. Season with salt and pepper to taste.

4. Fill the Portobello Mushrooms:
   - Divide the crab filling evenly among the baked portobello mushroom caps, pressing the filling gently into each cap.
5. Bake the Stuffed Mushrooms:
   - Return the stuffed mushrooms to the oven and bake for another 12-15 minutes, or until the filling is heated through and the tops are golden brown.
6. Serve the Crab-Stuffed Portobello Mushrooms:
   - Remove the stuffed mushrooms from the oven.
   - Garnish with chopped fresh parsley or chives.
   - Serve hot with lemon wedges on the side for squeezing over the mushrooms.

Tips:

- Choose large and firm portobello mushrooms for this recipe to hold the crab stuffing well.
- Feel free to substitute lump crabmeat with claw meat or a combination of crabmeat and shrimp.
- Add a pinch of Old Bay seasoning or paprika to the crab filling for extra flavor.
- Serve these crab-stuffed portobello mushrooms as an appetizer or main course with a side salad or roasted vegetables.

Enjoy these delicious crab-stuffed portobello mushrooms as a flavorful and satisfying dish that's perfect for any occasion! The combination of tender mushrooms and savory crab filling is sure to impress your family and friends.

Salmon Caesar Salad

Ingredients:

For the Salmon:

- 2 salmon fillets (about 6 ounces each), skinless
- Salt and pepper, to taste
- 1 tablespoon olive oil
- 1 teaspoon lemon zest (optional)

For the Caesar Salad:

- 1 large head of romaine lettuce, washed and chopped
- 1/2 cup Caesar dressing (store-bought or homemade)
- 1/2 cup grated Parmesan cheese
- 1 cup croutons (store-bought or homemade)

For the Caesar Dressing (Homemade):

- 1/2 cup mayonnaise
- 2 tablespoons grated Parmesan cheese
- 1 tablespoon Dijon mustard
- 2 cloves garlic, minced
- 2 anchovy fillets, minced (or 1-2 teaspoons anchovy paste)
- 2 tablespoons freshly squeezed lemon juice
- 1 tablespoon Worcestershire sauce
- Salt and pepper, to taste

Instructions:

1. Prepare the Salmon:
    - Season the salmon fillets with salt, pepper, and olive oil. Optionally, sprinkle lemon zest over the fillets for added flavor.
    - Heat a grill pan or skillet over medium-high heat.
    - Cook the salmon fillets for about 4-5 minutes per side, or until cooked through and flaky. Alternatively, you can bake the salmon in the oven at 400°F (200°C) for 12-15 minutes.

- Remove the cooked salmon from heat and let it rest for a few minutes. Then, flake the salmon into bite-sized pieces.
2. Make the Caesar Dressing:
    - In a bowl, whisk together the mayonnaise, grated Parmesan cheese, Dijon mustard, minced garlic, minced anchovy fillets (or anchovy paste), lemon juice, Worcestershire sauce, salt, and pepper until smooth and well combined. Adjust seasoning to taste.
3. Assemble the Salad:
    - In a large mixing bowl, combine the chopped romaine lettuce with the Caesar dressing. Toss until the lettuce is evenly coated with dressing.
    - Add the grated Parmesan cheese and croutons to the bowl, and toss again to combine.
    - Divide the dressed salad onto individual plates or bowls.
4. Add the Salmon:
    - Arrange the flaked salmon pieces on top of each plated salad.
5. Serve the Salmon Caesar Salad:
    - Garnish with additional Parmesan cheese, croutons, and freshly ground black pepper, if desired.
    - Serve immediately and enjoy!

Tips:

- You can use store-bought Caesar dressing to save time, or prepare the homemade dressing for a fresher flavor.
- If you prefer a lighter version of Caesar dressing, you can substitute Greek yogurt or sour cream for some of the mayonnaise.
- Customize the salad by adding cherry tomatoes, sliced cucumbers, or avocado slices.
- Serve the salmon Caesar salad with lemon wedges on the side for squeezing over the salmon and salad.

This salmon Caesar salad is a satisfying and flavorful meal that's perfect for lunch or dinner. It combines the classic Caesar salad with the heartiness of salmon for a delicious and nutritious dish!

Thai Fish Curry with Seasonal Vegetables

Ingredients:

For the Curry:

- 1 pound firm white fish fillets (such as cod, halibut, or snapper), cut into chunks
- 1 tablespoon vegetable oil
- 3 tablespoons Thai red or green curry paste (adjust based on spice preference)
- 1 can (14 oz) coconut milk
- 1 cup chicken or vegetable broth
- 2 tablespoons fish sauce
- 1 tablespoon palm sugar or brown sugar (adjust to taste)
- Juice of 1 lime
- Salt, to taste
- Fresh cilantro leaves, for garnish
- Cooked jasmine rice, for serving

For the Vegetables (use seasonal options):

- 1 red bell pepper, sliced
- 1 green bell pepper, sliced
- 1 medium eggplant, cut into cubes
- 1 zucchini, sliced
- Handful of green beans, trimmed
- Other seasonal vegetables of choice (such as carrots, broccoli, or snap peas)

For the Curry Paste (if making from scratch):

- 3-4 Thai red or green chilies, chopped (adjust based on spice preference)
- 4 cloves garlic, minced
- 1 shallot, chopped
- 1 lemongrass stalk, finely sliced
- 1-inch piece of fresh ginger, peeled and chopped
- 1 tablespoon coriander seeds, toasted and ground
- 1 tablespoon cumin seeds, toasted and ground
- 1 teaspoon shrimp paste (optional)
- Zest of 1 lime

- 2 tablespoons vegetable oil

Instructions:

1. Prepare the Curry Paste (Skip if Using Store-Bought):
   - In a mortar and pestle or food processor, pound or blend together all the curry paste ingredients until smooth. Alternatively, use a store-bought Thai red or green curry paste.
2. Cook the Curry:
   - Heat the vegetable oil in a large skillet or wok over medium heat.
   - Add the curry paste to the pan and stir-fry for 1-2 minutes until fragrant.
   - Gradually pour in the coconut milk and chicken or vegetable broth, stirring to combine.
   - Bring the mixture to a simmer and let it cook for 5-7 minutes to allow the flavors to meld.
3. Add the Fish and Vegetables:
   - Add the sliced bell peppers, eggplant, zucchini, green beans, and any other seasonal vegetables to the curry sauce.
   - Simmer for another 8-10 minutes, or until the vegetables are tender and cooked to your liking.
4. Add the Fish and Seasonings:
   - Gently add the fish chunks to the simmering curry.
   - Cook for 5-7 minutes or until the fish is cooked through and flakes easily.
   - Stir in fish sauce, palm sugar (or brown sugar), lime juice, and salt to taste. Adjust the seasoning as needed.
5. Serve the Thai Fish Curry:
   - Spoon the Thai fish curry over cooked jasmine rice in serving bowls.
   - Garnish with fresh cilantro leaves.
   - Serve hot and enjoy!

Tips:

- Feel free to customize the vegetables based on what's in season or your preferences.
- Taste the curry sauce and adjust the spice level by adding more or less curry paste.
- For extra richness, you can use full-fat coconut milk.
- Serve the Thai fish curry with additional lime wedges and sliced Thai chili peppers for those who like it spicier.

- This curry can be made ahead of t me and reheated gently before serving, allowing the flavors to develop even more.

This Thai fish curry with seasonal vegetables is a delightful and comforting dish that's perfect for a family dinner or entertaining guests. Enjoy the rich and aromatic flavors of this curry with the freshness of seasonal vegetables!

Grilled Shrimp and Vegetable Skewers

Ingredients:

For the Shrimp Marinade:

- 1 pound large shrimp, peeled and deveined
- 3 tablespoons olive oil
- 2 cloves garlic, minced
- 1 tablespoon fresh lemon juice
- 1 teaspoon paprika
- 1/2 teaspoon cumin
- Salt and pepper, to taste

For the Vegetable Skewers:

- Assorted vegetables, such as cherry tomatoes, bell peppers (red, yellow, green), red onion, zucchini, and mushrooms, cut into chunks
- Wooden or metal skewers

For Serving (Optional):

- Fresh parsley or cilantro, chopped
- Lemon wedges

Instructions:

1. Prepare the Shrimp Marinade:
    - In a bowl, whisk together olive oil, minced garlic, fresh lemon juice, paprika, cumin, salt, and pepper.
    - Add the peeled and deveined shrimp to the marinade. Toss to coat the shrimp evenly.
    - Cover and refrigerate for at least 30 minutes to marinate.
2. Prepare the Vegetable Skewers:
    - If using wooden skewers, soak them in water for at least 30 minutes to prevent burning during grilling.
    - Thread the marinated shrimp and assorted vegetables onto skewers, alternating between shrimp and vegetables.
3. Grill the Skewers:

- Preheat the grill to medium-high heat.
- Place the shrimp and vegetable skewers on the grill.
- Grill for 2-3 minutes per side, or until the shrimp are pink and opaque, and the vegetables are charred and tender.
- Rotate the skewers as needed for even cooking.

4. Serve the Grilled Skewers:
    - Remove the grilled shrimp and vegetable skewers from the grill.
    - Transfer the skewers to a serving platter.
    - Garnish with chopped fresh parsley or cilantro.
    - Serve hot with lemon wedges on the side.

Tips:

- Use a variety of colorful vegetables for vibrant skewers. Cherry tomatoes, bell peppers, red onion, zucchini, and mushrooms work well.
- Feel free to customize the marinade by adding your favorite herbs or spices.
- If using wooden skewers, make sure to soak them in water beforehand to prevent burning on the grill.
- Serve the grilled shrimp and vegetable skewers with a side of rice, couscous, or a fresh salad for a complete meal.
- These skewers can also be served as an appetizer or party snack.
- Enjoy these delicious and flavorful grilled shrimp and vegetable skewers for your next outdoor gathering or barbecue! The combination of juicy shrimp and charred vegetables is sure to be a hit.

Teriyaki Glazed Black Cod

Ingredients:

- 4 black cod fillets (about 6 ounces each), skinless and boneless
- 1/2 cup soy sauce (low-sodium recommended)
- 1/4 cup mirin (Japanese sweet rice wine)
- 1/4 cup sake (Japanese rice wine)
- 2 tablespoons brown sugar
- 2 cloves garlic, minced
- 1 tablespoon grated fresh ginger
- 1 tablespoon cornstarch (optional, for thickening the glaze)
- 2 tablespoons water
- Toasted sesame seeds, for garnish
- Sliced green onions, for garnish
- Cooked white rice, for serving
- Steamed vegetables, such as broccoli or bok choy, for serving

Instructions:

1. Prepare the Teriyaki Sauce:
    - In a saucepan, combine soy sauce, mirin, sake, brown sugar, minced garlic, and grated ginger.
    - Bring the mixture to a simmer over medium heat, stirring occasionally to dissolve the sugar.
    - In a small bowl, mix cornstarch with water to create a slurry. Add the slurry to the saucepan and stir continuously until the sauce thickens slightly. Remove from heat and set aside.
2. Marinate the Black Cod:
    - Place the black cod fillets in a shallow dish or resealable plastic bag.
    - Pour half of the teriyaki sauce over the cod fillets, reserving the other half for glazing later.
    - Cover the dish or seal the bag and marinate the cod in the refrigerator for at least 30 minutes, up to 2 hours.
3. Cook the Black Cod:
    - Preheat the oven to 400°F (200°C).
    - Remove the black cod fillets from the marinade and discard the marinade.
    - Place the cod fillets on a baking sheet lined with parchment paper or lightly greased foil.

- Bake the cod for 12-15 minutes, or until the fish flakes easily with a fork and is cooked through.
4. Glaze the Cod:
    - While the cod is baking, transfer the reserved teriyaki sauce to a small saucepan.
    - Heat the sauce over medium heat until it thickens slightly and becomes glossy, about 3-4 minutes.
5. Serve the Teriyaki Glazed Black Cod:
    - Remove the cooked black cod from the oven.
    - Brush the thickened teriyaki glaze over the cod fillets.
    - Sprinkle with toasted sesame seeds and sliced green onions for garnish.
    - Serve the teriyaki glazed black cod hot with steamed rice and your choice of steamed vegetables.

Tips:

- Black cod is known for its buttery texture and mild flavor, making it ideal for this dish. However, you can also use other types of white fish such as halibut or sea bass.
- Adjust the sweetness and saltiness of the teriyaki sauce to your preference by adding more or less brown sugar or soy sauce.
- Be careful not to overcook the black cod to prevent it from becoming dry. The fish should be opaque and easily flake with a fork when done.
- Garnish the dish with fresh cilantro or sliced red chilies for added flavor and color.
- Enjoy this teriyaki glazed black cod with a side of steamed rice and vegetables for a complete and satisfying meal!

Smoked Salmon and Avocado Toast

Ingredients:

- Slices of your favorite bread (such as whole grain, sourdough, or rye)
- Ripe avocados
- Smoked salmon slices
- Lemon juice
- Salt and pepper
- Optional toppings: sliced red onion, capers, fresh dill, microgreens, or radishes

Instructions:

1. Prepare the Avocado Spread:
    - In a bowl, mash ripe avocados with a fork until smooth and creamy.
    - Add a squeeze of fresh lemon juice to the mashed avocado to prevent browning and add a bright flavor.
    - Season the avocado spread with salt and pepper to taste.
2. Toast the Bread:
    - Toast slices of your favorite bread until golden brown and crispy. You can use a toaster, toaster oven, or grill pan for this step.
3. Assemble the Smoked Salmon and Avocado Toast:
    - Spread a generous amount of the mashed avocado onto each slice of toasted bread.
    - Arrange slices of smoked salmon on top of the avocado spread.
4. Add Optional Toppings:
    - Customize your smoked salmon and avocado toast by adding sliced red onion, capers, fresh dill, microgreens, or thinly sliced radishes on top of the salmon.
5. Serve and Enjoy:
    - Serve the smoked salmon and avocado toast immediately.
    - Garnish with additional freshly cracked black pepper and a squeeze of lemon juice, if desired.

Tips:

- Choose high-quality smoked salmon for the best flavor and texture.
- Use ripe avocados that are soft but not overly mushy for a creamy avocado spread.

- Experiment with different types of bread, such as whole grain, sourdough, or rye, to suit your taste preferences.
- Feel free to customize the toppings based on what you have on hand or your favorite flavor combinations.
- This smoked salmon and avocado toast pairs well with a side salad or a cup of soup for a complete meal.
- Enjoy this delicious and nutritious dish for breakfast, brunch, or any time of the day! It's quick and easy to make, yet impressive and satisfying.

Pesto Grilled Shrimp Pasta

Ingredients:

For the Pesto:

- 2 cups fresh basil leaves, packed
- 1/2 cup grated Parmesan cheese
- 1/2 cup pine nuts or walnuts, toasted
- 2 cloves garlic, minced
- 1/2 cup extra-virgin olive oil
- Salt and pepper, to taste

For the Grilled Shrimp:

- 1 pound large shrimp, peeled and deveined
- 2 tablespoons olive oil
- Salt and pepper, to taste

For the Pasta:

- 12 ounces pasta (such as spaghetti, linguine, or fettuccine)
- Reserved pasta cooking water
- Additional grated Parmesan cheese, for serving
- Fresh basil leaves, for garnish

Instructions:

1. Make the Pesto:
    - In a food processor or blender, combine basil leaves, grated Parmesan cheese, toasted pine nuts or walnuts, and minced garlic.
    - Pulse until the ingredients are finely chopped.
    - With the motor running, slowly drizzle in the olive oil until the pesto is smooth and well combined.
    - Season with salt and pepper to taste. Set aside.
2. Prepare the Grilled Shrimp:
    - Preheat a grill or grill pan over medium-high heat.
    - In a bowl, toss the peeled and deveined shrimp with olive oil, salt, and pepper.

- Thread the shrimp onto skewers (if using wooden skewers, soak them in water for 30 minutes before grilling to prevent burning).
- Grill the shrimp for 2-3 minutes per side, or until pink and cooked through. Remove from heat and set aside.
3. Cook the Pasta:
    - Cook the pasta in a large pot of salted boiling water according to package instructions until al dente.
    - Before draining the pasta, reserve about 1 cup of the pasta cooking water.
    - Drain the pasta and return it to the pot.
4. Assemble the Pesto Grilled Shrimp Pasta:
    - Add the homemade pesto to the cooked pasta in the pot. Toss to coat the pasta evenly with the pesto sauce, adding reserved pasta cooking water as needed to loosen the sauce.
    - Gently fold in the grilled shrimp until they are distributed throughout the pasta.
5. Serve the Pesto Grilled Shrimp Pasta:
    - Divide the pesto grilled shrimp pasta among serving plates or bowls.
    - Garnish with additional grated Parmesan cheese and fresh basil leaves.
    - Serve hot and enjoy!

Tips:

- Customize the pesto by adding a squeeze of fresh lemon juice or a pinch of red pepper flakes for extra flavor.
- Feel free to use store-bought pesto if you're short on time.
- You can also add additional vegetables to the pasta, such as cherry tomatoes, baby spinach, or roasted red peppers.
- Serve this pesto grilled shrimp pasta with a side salad and crusty bread for a complete meal.
- This dish is perfect for a weeknight dinner or special occasion. It's quick, easy, and bursting with delicious flavors!

Baked Stuffed Clams with Bacon

Ingredients:

- 24 littleneck clams, scrubbed clean
- 6 slices bacon, diced
- 1/2 cup finely diced onion
- 1/2 cup finely diced red bell pepper
- 2 cloves garlic, minced
- 1/2 cup breadcrumbs (preferably panko)
- 1/4 cup grated Parmesan cheese
- 2 tablespoons chopped fresh parsley
- 1 tablespoon fresh lemon juice
- Salt and pepper, to taste
- Lemon wedges, for serving
- Chopped fresh parsley, for garnish

Instructions:

1. Prepare the Clams:
     - Preheat your oven to 375°F (190°C).
     - Place the scrubbed clams in a large pot with about 1 inch of water. Cover the pot and steam the clams over medium-high heat for 5-7 minutes, or until the clams open.
     - Remove the clams from the pot and let them cool slightly. Discard any clams that do not open.
2. Remove and Chop Clam Meat:
     - Once the clams are cool enough to handle, remove the clam meat from the shells. Discard the top shells and reserve the bottom shells.
     - Chop the clam meat into small pieces and set aside.
3. Cook the Bacon and Vegetables:
     - In a skillet, cook the diced bacon over medium heat until crispy.
     - Remove the cooked bacon with a slotted spoon and set aside on a plate lined with paper towels.
     - In the same skillet with the bacon drippings, add the finely diced onion and red bell pepper. Cook for 3-4 minutes until softened.
     - Add the minced garlic to the skillet and cook for an additional 1 minute. Remove from heat.
4. Prepare the Stuffing Mixture:

- In a mixing bowl, combine the cooked chopped clams, cooked bacon, sautéed onion, red bell pepper, and garlic.
- Add breadcrumbs, grated Parmesan cheese, chopped fresh parsley, and fresh lemon juice to the bowl. Mix well to combine.
- Season the mixture with salt and pepper to taste.
5. Stuff the Clam Shells:
    - Arrange the reserved clam shells on a baking sheet.
    - Spoon the clam mixture evenly into each clam shell, pressing gently to pack the filling.
6. Bake the Stuffed Clams:
    - Place the baking sheet with the stuffed clam shells in the preheated oven.
    - Bake for 12-15 minutes, or until the filling is golden brown and heated through.
7. Serve the Baked Stuffed Clams:
    - Remove the baked stuffed clams from the oven.
    - Garnish with chopped fresh parsley.
    - Serve hot with lemon wedges on the side.

Tips:

- Make sure to use fresh littleneck clams for the best flavor.
- You can prepare the stuffing mixture ahead of time and refrigerate until ready to use.
- Serve these baked stuffed clams as an appetizer or pair them with a salad for a delicious main course.
- Enjoy these flavorful baked stuffed clams with bacon for a delightful seafood treat that's perfect for any occasion!

Spicy Tuna Lettuce Wraps

Ingredients:

- 2 cans (5 oz each) tuna in water, drained
- 1/4 cup mayonnaise (adjust amount based on preference)
- 1 tablespoon Sriracha sauce (adjust to taste)
- 1 tablespoon soy sauce
- 1 tablespoon rice vinegar
- 1 teaspoon sesame oil
- 2 green onions, finely chopped
- 1/2 red bell pepper, finely diced
- 1/4 cup chopped cilantro (optional)
- Salt and pepper, to taste
- Butter lettuce leaves (or other large lettuce leaves), washed and separated
- Lime wedges, for serving

Instructions:

1. Prepare the Tuna Salad:
    - In a mixing bowl, combine drained tuna, mayonnaise, Sriracha sauce, soy sauce, rice vinegar, and sesame oil.
    - Stir in chopped green onions, diced red bell pepper, and chopped cilantro (if using).
    - Mix well to combine all ingredients.
    - Taste the tuna salad and season with salt and pepper as needed.
2. Assemble the Lettuce Wraps:
    - Spoon a portion of the spicy tuna salad onto each lettuce leaf, towards the center.
    - Fold the sides of the lettuce leaf over the tuna salad, then roll it up to create a wrap.
3. Serve the Spicy Tuna Lettuce Wraps:
    - Arrange the lettuce wraps on a serving platter.
    - Garnish with additional chopped cilantro and lime wedges on the side.
    - Serve immediately and enjoy!

Tips:

- Adjust the amount of Sriracha sauce to control the level of spiciness in the tuna salad.

- Feel free to add other crunchy vegetables such as shredded carrots, cucumber, or jicama for extra texture and flavor.
- Substitute mayonnaise with Greek yogurt or avocado for a lighter option.
- Serve these spicy tuna lettuce wraps as a light lunch, appetizer, or part of a healthy dinner.
- Customize the wraps by adding sliced avocado, sesame seeds, or a drizzle of extra Sriracha sauce for an extra kick.
- These lettuce wraps are best enjoyed fresh but can be refrigerated for a few hours before serving. If preparing in advance, store the tuna salad separately from the lettuce leaves and assemble just before serving.

These spicy tuna lettuce wraps are a flavorful and satisfying dish that's easy to make and perfect for a quick meal. Enjoy the combination of spicy tuna salad wrapped in crisp lettuce leaves for a delightful eating experience!

Mediterranean Tuna Salad

Ingredients:

- 2 cans (5 oz each) tuna in water, drained
- 1 cup cherry tomatoes, halved
- 1/2 English cucumber, diced
- 1/4 cup red onion, finely chopped
- 1/4 cup Kalamata olives, pitted and sliced
- 1/4 cup crumbled feta cheese
- 2 tablespoons chopped fresh parsley
- 2 tablespoons extra-virgin olive oil
- 1 tablespoon red wine vinegar
- Juice of 1/2 lemon
- Salt and pepper, to taste
- Romaine lettuce leaves or mixed salad greens, for serving
- Lemon wedges, for garnish

Instructions:

1. Prepare the Tuna Salad:
    - In a large mixing bowl, flake the drained tuna with a fork.
    - Add cherry tomatoes, diced cucumber, chopped red onion, sliced Kalamata olives, crumbled feta cheese, and chopped fresh parsley to the bowl.
2. Make the Dressing:
    - In a small bowl or jar, whisk together extra-virgin olive oil, red wine vinegar, lemon juice, salt, and pepper to make the dressing.
3. Assemble the Mediterranean Tuna Salad:
    - Pour the dressing over the tuna and vegetable mixture.
    - Gently toss everything together until well combined and coated with the dressing.
    - Taste and adjust seasoning with salt and pepper, if needed.
4. Serve the Salad:
    - Arrange romaine lettuce leaves or mixed salad greens on serving plates.
    - Spoon the Mediterranean tuna salad onto the lettuce leaves.
    - Garnish with lemon wedges and additional chopped parsley, if desired.

Tips:

- You can customize this salad by adding other Mediterranean ingredients such as chopped artichoke hearts, roasted red peppers, or sliced red bell peppers.
- Serve this Mediterranean tuna salad on its own, or with crusty bread or pita for a complete meal.
- This salad can be prepared in advance and refrigerated until serving. Just wait to add the dressing until right before serving to keep the vegetables crisp.
- Feel free to substitute canned tuna with cooked and flaked fresh tuna or grilled tuna steaks for a different texture and flavor.
- Enjoy this Mediterranean tuna salad as a light and satisfying meal that's bursting with fresh flavors! It's perfect for picnics, potlucks, or quick weekday lunches.

Seared Ahi Tuna with Wasabi Aioli

Ingredients:

For the Seared Ahi Tuna:

- 2 sushi-grade ahi tuna steaks (about 6-8 ounces each), approximately 1 inch thick
- Salt and black pepper, to taste
- 1 tablespoon sesame oil
- Optional: sesame seeds for coating

For the Wasabi Aioli:

- 1/4 cup mayonnaise
- 1 tablespoon soy sauce
- 1 tablespoon rice vinegar
- 1-2 teaspoons wasabi paste (adjust to taste)
- 1 clove garlic, minced
- 1 teaspoon sesame oil

For Serving:

- Sliced green onions or chives, for garnish
- Optional: pickled ginger, soy sauce, or extra wasabi for serving

Instructions:

1. Prepare the Wasabi Aioli:
    - In a small bowl, whisk together mayonnaise, soy sauce, rice vinegar, wasabi paste (start with 1 teaspoon and adjust to your desired level of spiciness), minced garlic, and sesame oil.
    - Taste and adjust seasoning as needed. Cover and refrigerate until ready to serve.
2. Prepare the Ahi Tuna:
    - Pat the ahi tuna steaks dry with paper towels.
    - Season both sides of the tuna steaks generously with salt and black pepper.

- Optionally, coat the tuna steaks with sesame seeds by pressing the seeds onto all sides of the tuna.
3. Sear the Ahi Tuna:
    - Heat sesame oil in a skillet or grill pan over high heat until very hot.
    - Carefully place the seasoned tuna steaks in the hot skillet.
    - Sear the tuna for 1-2 minutes on each side for rare doneness, or adjust cooking time based on your preference (sear longer for medium-rare or medium).
4. Slice and Serve:
    - Remove the seared ahi tuna from the skillet and let it rest for a few minutes on a cutting board.
    - Slice the tuna steaks into thin slices using a sharp knife.
5. Serve with Wasabi Aioli:
    - Arrange the sliced seared ahi tuna on a serving platter or individual plates.
    - Drizzle the prepared wasabi aioli over the tuna slices or serve it on the side for dipping.
    - Garnish with sliced green onions or chives.
6. Enjoy:
    - Serve the seared ahi tuna with wasabi aioli immediately, accompanied by optional sides like pickled ginger, soy sauce, or extra wasabi.

Tips:

- Use high-quality sushi-grade ahi tuna for the best results.
- Adjust the amount of wasabi paste in the aioli according to your preference for spiciness.
- Be careful not to overcook the ahi tuna to preserve its tender texture.
- Serve this dish as an appetizer or main course with a side of steamed rice and stir-fried vegetables for a complete meal.
- Enjoy the delicate flavors of seared ahi tuna with creamy wasabi aioli in this impressive and delicious dish!

Baked Cod with Herbed Quinoa

Ingredients:

For the Baked Cod:

- 4 cod fillets (6 oz each), skinless and boneless
- Salt and black pepper, to taste
- 2 tablespoons olive oil
- 2 cloves garlic, minced
- 1 tablespoon fresh lemon juice
- 1 teaspoon lemon zest
- 1 tablespoon chopped fresh parsley
- Lemon wedges, for serving

For the Herbed Quinoa:

- 1 cup quinoa, rinsed
- 2 cups vegetable or chicken broth
- 1 tablespoon olive oil
- 2 cloves garlic, minced
- 2 tablespoons chopped fresh parsley
- 1 tablespoon chopped fresh dill (or 1 teaspoon dried dill)
- Salt and black pepper, to taste

Instructions:

1. Preheat the Oven:
    - Preheat your oven to 400°F (200°C).
2. Prepare the Baked Cod:
    - Pat the cod fillets dry with paper towels.
    - Season both sides of the cod fillets with salt and black pepper.
    - Place the cod fillets in a baking dish lightly greased with olive oil.
3. Prepare the Lemon Garlic Marinade:
    - In a small bowl, whisk together olive oil, minced garlic, fresh lemon juice, lemon zest, and chopped parsley.
    - Pour the marinade over the cod fillets, coating them evenly.
4. Bake the Cod:

- Bake the cod fillets in the preheated oven for 12-15 minutes, or until the fish is opaque and flakes easily with a fork.

5. Prepare the Herbed Quinoa:
    - While the cod is baking, prepare the herbed quinoa.
    - In a saucepan, heat olive oil over medium heat.
    - Add minced garlic and sauté for about 1 minute until fragrant.
    - Add rinsed quinoa to the saucepan and stir to coat with the garlic-infused oil.
    - Pour in vegetable or chicken broth and bring to a boil.
    - Reduce the heat to low, cover, and simmer for 15-20 minutes, or until the quinoa is cooked and fluffy.

6. Finish the Herbed Quinoa:
    - Once the quinoa is cooked, fluff it with a fork.
    - Stir in chopped fresh parsley, chopped fresh dill, salt, and black pepper to taste.

7. Serve the Baked Cod with Herbed Quinoa:
    - Divide the herbed quinoa among serving plates.
    - Place a baked cod fillet on top of each serving of quinoa.
    - Garnish with additional fresh herbs and serve with lemon wedges on the side.

Tips:

- Feel free to customize the herbed quinoa by adding other fresh herbs like basil or cilantro.
- Serve this dish with steamed vegetables such as green beans, broccoli, or asparagus for a complete meal.
- You can use other types of white fish such as halibut or haddock instead of cod if preferred.
- Enjoy this baked cod with herbed quinoa for a wholesome and satisfying dinner that's packed with protein and flavor!